RE-EVALUATING US FOREIGN POLICY TOWARDS ASIA

Editors

D.S. Rajan, R.S. Vasan and J.A. Bonofer

Chennai Centre for China Studies
Chennai

Centre for Asia Studies
Chennai

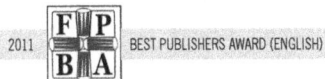
KNOWLEDGE WORLD

KW Publishers Pvt Ltd
New Delhi

2011 · BEST PUBLISHERS AWARD (ENGLISH)

![KW logo]

KW Publishers Pvt Ltd

4676/21, First Floor, Ansari Road, Daryaganj, New Delhi 110002

Email: knowledgeworld@vsnl.net Tel.: +91.11.23263498/43528107

www.kwpub.com

ISBN 978–93–81904–70–1

Contents

Preface

The book marks the publication of the edited volume of the proceedings of a National Seminar on 'Re-Evaluating US Foreign Policy towards Asia', organised jointly by the Chennai Centre for China Studies (C3S),Center for Asia Studies (CAS), and the University of Madras (Department of Politics and Public Administration) at Chennai on January 09, 2012. The participants included eminent Sinologists in the country representing the academic community, former bureaucrats who covered China as part of their duties, and experts with security and military background. The book is being brought out with the objective of ensuring wider dissemination of their views.

The C3S is a non-profit public policy think tank established in Chennai in 2007; it devotes exclusively to China Studies. Its objectives include carrying out in-depth study of developments relating to China with priority to issues of concern to India, offering workable solutions/policy alternatives based on studies to the strategic planners and decision-makers in India on the questions of bilateral, regional, and global importance, providing a forum for dialogue with China scholars in India and abroad, giving space for expression of alternate opinions on China related topics, and creating a sound database for research on China with special attention to tapping information available in Chinese language material published in China. The website of the C3S www.c3sindia.org provides a channel for specialists in India and abroad to closely examine and exchange ideas on relevant issues. The C3S has B.S. Raghavan, IAS (Retd), former Advisor to the UN, as Patron and its office-bearers include well known academicians, former high level bureaucrats who dealt with China, and persons with rich military and security expertise.

The CAS focuses on analysis of developments in the fields of contemporary Asian economy, politics, security and strategy, and provides a forum for specialists in these areas to analyse these issues dispassionately and assist in policy making. During the last four years of its existence, it has already made a distinct mark in the intellectual life of South India through its publications, lecture–discussions, and seminars. It is headed by Dr. S. Narayan, IAS (Retd) and former Economic Advisor to the Government of India, with a faculty comprising capable academicians and area specialists.

The papers presented in the seminar have covered important aspects of US-China Relations, and their impact on India, which is responding to China's rise. We are sure of their usefulness as inputs to the policymakers in the country.

The organisers feel indebted to a number of persons and organisations for their valuable assistance in holding of the National Seminar. Deserving special thanks in this regard are Prof. Ramu Manivannan and his colleagues in the Department of Politics and Public Administration, University of Madras. We are grateful to the university for providing us the venue for the seminar and making other necessary arrangements. We thank all the resource persons, especially from outside Chennai who took part in the seminar as well as the CAS staff including Ashik Bonofer and A. Pramila for their able administrative support.

We express our thanks to M/s. K.W. Publishers Pvt. Ltd., New Delhi, for bringing out this book.

D.S. Rajan

Editor

Contributors

Mr. **B.S. Raghavan** joined the West Bengal IAS cadre in 1952, and was Commissioner in various Departments. He also served as the Chief Secretary of West Bengal and Tripura. He was Director for political and security Policy Planning in the Union Home Ministry, and the Secretary, National Integration Council during the period of the first four Prime Ministers of India. He was a US Congressional Fellow and Policy Adviser to the UN (FAO), and Chairman of three UN Committees. He has been chief executive of four major public sector enterprises. He is now a columnist and author, connected with social service and educational organisations. He is presently the Patron of the Chennai Centre for China Studies and Treasurer, Rajaji Centre for Public Affairs in Chennai.

Amb. **C.V. Ranganathan**, IFS (Retd) received education in Madras University and joined the Indian Foreign Service in 1959. He served the Government of India with great distinction in Beijing, New Delhi, Bonn, Hongkong, Ethiopia, Moscow, and Paris. He was Jawaharlal Nehru Fellow during 1998-2000, Convenor, National Security Advisory Board of the Government of India from 2000-03, Co-chairman of India-China Eminent Persons Group, Co-author with V.C. Khanna on "India and China - The Way Head" and contributor to several books and journals. He is presently the Chairman of the core group on China in the Indian Council of World Affairs (ICWA), member of the Governing Council of the IIT-Madras China Study Centre, and Vice-President of the Chennai Centre for China Studies.

Mr. **B. Raman**, IPS (Retd) joined the Indian Police Service in 1961. He served In Madhya Pradesh as a police officer from 1962 to July 1967, in the Intelligence Bureau from July 1967 to September 1968, and in the R&AW from September 1968 to August 1994. He retired as Additional Secretary on August 31, 1994. He was a member of the National Security Advisory Board of the Government of India from 2000-02. He is now Director, Institute for

Topical Studies, Chennai, and an Associate of the Chennai Centre for China Studies.

Mr. **N. Narasimhan**, IPS (Retd) belongs to the Karnataka Cadre and served in the Government of the India from 1961-93, in the Intelligence Bureau from 1961-67, and in the R&AW from 1967. He was Director General of Security, and Secretary in the Cabinet Secretariat as well as former Member of the National Security Advisory Board, Government of India.

Prof. **K.P. Vijayalakshmi** is Chairperson, Centre for Canadian, US and Latin American Studies, SIS, Jawaharlal Nehru University, New Delhi, with 21 years of experience. Her qualifications include Ph.D and M.Phil in American Studies, and MA in Centre for Political Studies—all from SIS, Jawaharlal Nehru University, New Delhi. Her areas of interest are the US Government and Politics, Foreign policy formulation, patterns and process, Indo-US Relations and Prospects for Scientific Cooperation, US strategies and policies in South Asia, Indian Diaspora, and Comprehensive and Non-traditional security.

Dr. **V. Suryanarayan** is one of India's leading specialists in South and Southeast Asian Studies, and brings to bear in his teaching and research keen insights in history, political science, and international relations. For more than two decades, he was associated with the Centre for South and Southeast Asian Studies, University of Madras, first as the founding Director, and later, as Senior Professor. He was a Visiting Professor, Department of History, University of California, Los Angeles; Columbus College, University System of Georgia; Peradeniya University, Sri Lanka, and School of international Studies, Jawaharlal Nehru University, Calicut. He is currently President, Chennai Centre for China Studies. He was a member of the National Security Advisory Board, Government of India. His major publications, including edited volumes, are *Singapore: Path to independence* (1978); *Sri Lanka Crisis and India's Response* (1991); *South and Southeast Asia in the 1990s: Indian and American Perspectives* (1992); *Andaman And Nicobar Islands—Challenges of Development*

(1994); *Kanchchativu and the Problems of Indian Fishermen in the Palk Bay Region* (1994); *Between Fear and Hope - Sri Lankan Refugees in Tamil Nadu* (2000); *Conflict Over Fisheries in the Palk Bay Region* (2005) and Kachchatheevum India Meenavarum (Tamil/2009); Malaysia India Tamizharkalin Avala Nilai (Tamil/2010); *Ethnic Reconciliation and Nation Building in Sri Lanka: Indian Perspectives* (2010), and *Refugee Situation in India Today* (2011). In addition, he has contributed more than fifty chapters in edited volumes, and more than 100 articles in leading research journals.

Mr. **Kandaswami Subramanian** retired as the Joint Secretary, Ministry of Finance, Government of India. He has a long experience in handling economic (multilateral and bilateral) issues, and participated in a number of joint commissions. After retirement, he devotes his time for research and writing articles for newspapers like The Hindu, Business Line, Economic and Political Weekly, and various websites like the South Asia Analysis group and Chennai Centre for China Studies. He is an Associate of the Chennai Centre for China studies, India.

Amb. **Saurabh Kumar** retired from the Indian Foreign Service as the Ambassador to the International Atomic Energy Agency, United Nations Industrial Development Organization and the UN Offices in Vienna (Outer Space Affairs, Drugs and Crime), and to Austria in October 2009. Prior to this, he served as the Ambassador to Ireland (2003-07) and to Vietnam (2000-03). His areas of specialisation during his tenure in the Government of India were nuclear as well as disarmament and international security issues. He was a member of the Indian delegation to the Third Special Session of the UN General Assembly on Disarmament in 1988, and to the UN Conference on the Relationship between Disarmament and Development in 1987. He speaks Chinese, having begun his diplomatic career in Hong Kong and Beijing in the mid-1970s under late President K.R. Narayanan, who was then the Ambassador to China. Apart from continuing professional interest in China (and nuclear, space, and other strategic security issues and multilateral international affairs in general), his current academic interests include development economics and international economic relations, the negotiation process, physics and psychology. A Gold Medalist from the Delhi University, he taught Physics at the Ramjas College, University of Delhi prior to joining the Indian Foreign Service in 1973. He was a doctoral candidate (Fellows Programme in Management) in the Economics area of the Indian Institute of Management, Ahmedabad during 1981-84, on leave from the IFS. He was a member of the Informal Group on the 1988 Action Plan for a Nuclear Weapon Free and Non-violent World chaired by Hon'ble Mani Shankar Aiyar, MP, which was formed in December 2010 at the instance of the Prime Minister, and which submitted its Report to him in August 2011.

1

Opening Remarks

B.S. Raghavan

Jigsaw Pieces of the US-Asia Policy

One can do no better than refer, at the very beginning, to the building blocks of the US policy on Asia as set out by the US Secretary of State, Ms. Hillary Clinton, in the course of 2011 in her two landmark speeches at the East-West Centre, Honolulu (January), and at Chennai, India (July), and in her Op-Ed in the Foreign Policy magazine (October). Although she uses Asia and Asia-Pacific as interchangeable terms in defining American goals in that part of the world, it is clear that, in the US perspective, it is Asia-Pacific, rather than Asia as a stand-alone entity that counts as the basis for applying an overall policy prescription.

It is by no means a distinction without a difference. It implies, as Ms. Clinton herself has underscored, a continuing as well as a compulsive obligation to look to the US interests across the Indian and Pacific oceans and weave them into a harmonious policy fabric.

Next, by the use of the double-barrelled expression, the US is subtly seeking to assert and extend its influence over a vast geographical expanse covered by the two oceans, encompassing close to 20 countries (Australia, Brunei, China, India, Indonesia, Japan, Malaysia, Mongolia, Myanmar, New Zealand, the Pacific Islands, Pakistan, the Philippines, Singapore, South Korea, Sri Lanka, Taiwan, Thailand, and Vietnam).

They are home to half the world's population, all set to become the driving force of the global economy, with shipping lanes busy transporting the bulk of world's merchant tonnage, offering fast expanding markets and insatiable and insatiate demand for an infinite volume and variety of goods and services, and with practically unlimited, and hitherto relatively unexploited, scope for trade, investment and exports.

Tight-Rope Walking

Strategically too, as Ms. Clinton puts it, for the US, "Maintaining peace and security across the Asia-Pacific is increasingly crucial to global progress, whether through defending freedom of navigation in the South China Sea, countering the proliferation efforts of North Korea, or ensuring transparency in the military activities of the region's key players."

These and other formulations sprinkled across a number of official documents go to show that the US construes its Asia policy as a component, though a pivotal one, of 'a broader effort to ensure a more comprehensive approach to American strategy and engagement in the region', paving the way to entering into partnerships and alliances to that end. This also requires the US necessarily to do some tight-rope walking in view of the bewildering political, economic and institutional diversities, complicated by divergent interests, characterising the countries of Asia-Pacific.

This means opting for the exercise of 'soft power' with emphasis on persuasion and consensus, and being sensitive to the concerns of the different countries of the region. In this sense, the US-Asia policy is a jigsaw whose pieces are yet to fall in place.

In regard to China, in particular, the US has forcefully affirmed that a thriving America is good for China just as much as a thriving China is good for America, and flatly rejected the thesis of American hardliners that China's progress is a threat to the US as seen from their standpoint and that the US, therefore, should pursue a countervailing policy of containment or, if unavoidable, confrontation.

Retaliatory Action

On the other hand, a report under the title *Sustaining US Global Leadership: Priorities for 21st Century* prepared by the US Department of Defence (DoD) and released by President Barack Obama himself on January 05, 2012 by making a rare appearance at the Pentagon, takes a less optimistic position. It makes no bones about the US economy and security being affected over the long haul in a variety of ways by China's emergence as a regional power. The report stridently demands that 'the growth of China's military power must be accompanied by greater clarity of its strategic intentions in order to avoid causing friction in the region'.

An earlier DoD document had reserved for the US the right of 'retaliatory action' with military force against China for the cyber-war it is supposed to have unleashed against the US, aimed at throwing its industry and infrastructure into chaos. What form such retaliation can or will take is not clear, but the fact of mutually irreconcilable postures of the Departments of State and Defence is sufficient evidence of the prevailing ambivalence the US Administration with respect to China.

US-Asia Policy is Work-in-Progress

The ambivalence in the US attitude towards China stems from that country having a stranglehold over the US as the biggest foreign creditor with US$ 1.5 trillion in American government debt. Its prodigious trade and current-account surpluses have made it a financial giant with foreign currency reserves exceeding US$ 3 trillion, unsurpassed by any other nation. It is also closer than the US to the countries of the Asia-Pacific region geographically, historically and culturally and can, if it sets its mind to it, outpace the US in forging networks of alliances by dangling a range of tempting offers in the form of collaborations, projects and financial assistance.

In any case, confrontation, leave alone retaliation with military force, cannot any longer be the solution in world affairs. The days are long past when the ugly American or the cowboy style of arm twisting, browbeating, and saber-rattling or the actual use of force would have done the trick. In the current context, all that the US can do is to mask in diplomatic verbiage its real intention to somehow keep China in check and look for proxies through whom it could finesse whatever hidden agenda it has.

Hence, the eagerness to embrace India in an all-encompassing strategic partnership, and build it up as a 'regional economic anchor and provider of security in the broader Indian Ocean region', with the expectation of making it, at one level, an effective counterpoise to China and at another, the lightning rod for absorbing any shocks generated in the process.

Unnatural Bundling

Hence, the insistent call by the US urging India to play a more vigorous leadership role as the 'linchpin' of the broader Asia-Pacific region, and go beyond its languid 'Look East' policy to a dashing 'Act East' policy. The US, no doubt, hopes that to a considerable extent, this will lighten its load in making China soften its stand on contentious issues such as political and economic liberalisation, cyber war, intellectual property protection, maritime security and human rights.

Of late, the US has begun to bracket India with Indonesia with equal praise for both as 'two of the most dynamic and significant democratic powers of Asia' with which it wants to have 'broader, deeper, and more purposeful relationships'. It gives a number of reasons to justify this unnatural bundling, but, to me, the real reason is that the US considers it impolitic to seem like leaning on India (in both the British and American senses of the phrase) exclusively, excessively or too obviously.

If the US foreign policy makers are smart enough, they will not be still willing to put up with Pakistan's brazen and perfidious prevarications, its continued dalliance with China and its total loss of credibility from the time Osama bin Laden was found ensconced in the prominent military cantonment of Abbottabad right under the noses of the military brass. There is certainly enough indication of Pakistan being in the dog house in their reckoning. It cannot be mere coincidence that no explicit reference to US-Pakistan relations occurs in any of the policy pronouncements made by the US from public platforms after its daring exploit of eliminating Osama by caring two hoots for Pakistan's sovereignty and international law.

Sleepless Nights

However, the US is on a cleft stick with respect to Pakistan. It can neither write it off nor go on pouring billions of dollars into that bottomless pit. There is also the imperative need to guard against Pakistan's nuclear assets falling into terrorist hands—a danger of truly unthinkable proportions. Pakistan must be giving the US sleepless nights.

With so many uncertainties and complexities bedevilling the region, the US has not yet worked out with clarity all the implications of an ambitious forward thrust. The region further bristles with hot spots that are apt to flare up. The US quest of a coherent, balanced and durable Asia policy, whether in itself or as an adjunct of an Asia-Pacific policy, is yet to be over. At the moment, its best bet lies in focusing on the crystallisation and consolidation of relationships with China, India, and Japan, and use the resulting leverage to hammer out a full-fledged and definitive Asia-Pacific policy.

2
Re-evaluating American Foreign Policy

C.V. Ranganathan

The holding of this Seminar on the subject of re-evaluating American Foreign Policy is timely in view of the defence strategic review held a few days back in Washington. President Obama is reported to have made many policy announcements with regard to future American policies towards Asia. While the focus of one of the sponsors of this Seminar may be China, they rightly believe in the adage that 'they know not China who only knows China'. Over the last three decades, China's growth has been predicated on close interdependence with the rest of the world and the details of this are well known. Both the US and China view their bilateral relations and the impact of these on the rest of the world in general and on Asia in particular as the most important relationship to each of them and to the world at large. Given this perception held strongly by each of them, it is appropriate to start from the salient aspects of this defence strategic review followed by its possible impact on India.

As reported in the Indian Press, this review will face Asian countries with a decision by the US to 'pivot' to Asia. This apparently follows 'turning a page on a decade of war' (Iraq and Afghanistan). The maintenance of the US military superiority will in future be undertaken with armed forces that are agile, flexible, and ready for a full range of contingencies and threats. The new defence strategy would increasingly focus on Asia with a strengthening of American presence in the Asia-Pacific and planned budget reductions in other areas of the defence budget will not come at the expense of 'this critical region' in the words of the President. An expanded military role is envisaged while maintaining strong presence in the Middle East. The document mentions the challenge posed by a China growing economically and strengthening militarily. Iran also finds mention in the context of its nuclear posture. India is referred to in the context of strengthening Asian allies of the US. In brief, the US seems to have recommitted itself to existing security insurance policies with Asian countries where they exist and beefing these up where appropriate and as requested by partner countries.

The pivot to Asia statement was understandably welcomed by the Association of South East Asian Nations as a group (ASEAN) and by other Asian countries Japan, South Korea, and by Australia and New Zealand, etc. China's initial reaction was cautious hoping that the US would contribute to peace and stability in Asia and play a positive role warning against cold-war style zero sum mentality emerging. The dilemma for China's neighbors in Asia is to balance their overwhelming dependence on China for trade and investments with the material and psychological dependence on the US' military support in Asia, which is seen as a hedge against possible aggressive actions by China over the wide range of maritime territorial disputes. The former is a proven need while the latter is an unspoken requirement. The challenge for the Asian countries with which China has disputes over maritime jurisdictions is to defend their claims without having the means to make the Chinese abandon their claims except through collective diplomacy. The reported presence of abundant fossil fuels in the oceanic areas adjacent to the countries lends a critical edge to the problem of contested claims. Openly announced backing by the US to the sanctity of compliance with the international laws on the subject, and its concern that access to American vessels to all non-sovereign oceanic passages is available, ensure continued American involvement in maintenance of peace and stability in South East and East Asia. The emergence of expressions of strident nationalistic demands made in the Chinese internet and sections of its media when frictions occur over maritime disputes between China and neighbors is a reminder of the depth of sentiments over such issues in a strengthening China. However, no Asian country would like to see any sign of worsening relations between China and the US as indeed would these two countries.

Both the US and China are heirs to self-perceptions of their exceptional role in international affairs and feel that what is good for them is in general good for the world. Thus, on the American agenda in the conduct of relations with China, a series of issues ranging from respect for human rights in China, to trade disputes, to military modernisation, assistance to Taiwan and other issues such as climate change etc. constantly figure in the public discourse in the US. In the case of China particularly after the Western financial melt down from 2008, the feeling has developed that it is now timely that its global ambitions and entitlements, which have been historically denied, should be restored. This is a background which must be kept in view when one studies the management of the complex Sino-US relationship. In this scenario, the diplomatic challenge to the US is to balance the military leverage it enjoys with its political and diplomatic policies of engaging with China more deeply in the strategic, economic and other fields. In India, we should be fully aware that underlying Sino-US relations today is a nuanced debate where challenges coexist with the compulsions of deep interdependence for both countries. We should be cautious about the limits of the vaunted Indo-US strategic partnership where there are intersecting Indian, Chinese, and American interests.

Turning to India, its rise is perceived by the international community as non-threatening. From the first decade of this century the rapid growth of Indo-US relations and of relations with other major powers like Japan, Russia, China, and with major economic groupings like the EU, ASEAN, etc. have brought a qualitative change in India's global standing. A significant ingredient of this change is the welcome given by states in a wide arc from the Western end of the Indian Ocean to its eastern extremity to the operations of the Indian Navy. It is seen as a contributor to the maintenance of public goods in a wide area with regard to anti-piracy, anti-terrorism, provider of humanitarian relief in times of need and a vigilant guard of the essential sea lanes of communication. Public American expression of its expectations from India and its role in Asia was given in Chennai by the US Secretary of State Ms. Hillary Clinton in an address where she reportedly said, "India should not just look east, but to engage east and act east as well." The underlying assumption in such a statement appears to be that far from posing any threats to American security in South East and East Asia, India is encouraged to adopt more robust policies in these regions. The fact remains that over a decade before this statement was made, India has been both engaging and acting in developing bilateral relations with each of the

ASEAN countries as well as actively participating in their annual Summits as well as at the East Asia Summits. Through these interactions substantive and dense relationships have developed between India and the countries involved in political, security, trade, investments, technology, defence, and other fields.

The pivot to Asia statement with its reference to India confirms the American official perception of a critical role envisaged for India in international affairs. The phrase strategic partnership used by spokesmen of both sides to describe the relationship needs to be tested in relation to the evolving situations in India's near and extended neighbourhoods namely Iran, Afghanistan and Pakistan. It is evident that with regard to this neighborhood, the pursuit of Indian interests requires exercise of strategic autonomy and an independence of decisions which are different from the strategic congruence, which the US may seek. For instance on Iran, India is in agreement with the US on the undesirability of Iran acquiring nuclear weapons as it may lead to instability in West Asia. However, the geographical position of Iran is such that transit of India's trade through Eastern Iran to Afghanistan and beyond is of far reaching importance to India. Moreover, Iran's support to the political stability of Afghanistan free from foreign influence and Islamic Taliban style governance is vitally important to India. For these and reasons of Indo-Iranian age old links India is uncomfortable with the present standoff between the US and Iran, and would wish for a negotiated diplomatic solution to the nuclear issue involving Iran and the international community.

On Afghanistan, the desire of the American-led North Atlantic Treaty Organization (NATO) to withdraw completely the respective battle roles of NATO forces by 2014 seems irreversible. This is to be welcomed if Afghanistan's Army and Police are fully equipped and trained by then to maintain security and stability. For this it is necessary that the country as a whole fully reverts to its traditional independence, neutrality and its sovereignty is respected without any foreign interference. The role that India has played and will continue to play in that country is appreciated by the vast majority of the people and has also gained the respect of the US and the international community. On them lies the responsibility to see that in any negotiated political solution on the country's future, there is no risk of its reverting to a Talibanised state which prevailed before the 9/11 attacks on the World Trade Centre, New York.

As for Pakistan, a number of bloody incidents involving deaths of civilian as well as military personnel and the killing of Osama bin Laden have led to deep friction between the US and Pakistan. There is a near-paralysis in joint actions against cross border terrorism across the Pak-Afghan borders and logistic support for transit of goods across this border. A deep strategic distrust has crept into relations between Pakistan and the US. Public statements by American leaders that religious fundamentalism, militancy and terrorism would consume Pakistan itself reflect this distrust. There is little evidence to show any progress in back channel negotiations over the future political dispensation in Afghanistan for which there was reliance on Pakistan's establishment. It is doubtful if by 2014 the drug trade centred on Afghanistan will be significantly reduced or eliminated.

There have been very welcome developments in the bilateral dialogue between India and Pakistan with perceptible progress in opening up the enormous potential in the trade and mutual investment fields. The goodwill generated by this will have a good effect on the people on both sides but hard issues relating to political issues, security, water, Kashmir, etc. have yet to be addressed. Without tangible action on the Mumbai terrorists attacks and those behind these in Pakistan, the ogre of cross border terrorism cannot be laid to rest. It should be a matter of concern to the international community at large and India, the US and China in particular how the domestic political and social situation evolves in Pakistan. Can one confidently expect civil society there to overcome the challenges posed by ethnic grievances, armed militancy fuelled by religious fundamentalism, illiteracy, unemployment and poverty which feed anti-modern impulses and economic backwardness?

The shift of emphasis, if that is implied in the pivot to Asia policy of the US, comes at a difficult time for the US, which is caught up in the heat of the forthcoming elections to the office of the President of the US. The crisis in Europe in the European Union and the severe anti-establishment wave that is evident in the popular mood there further enfeebles the international economy. In West Asia, with few exceptions, popular revolutions against authoritarian rulers are yet to result in the emergence of stable political dispensations. All these factors contribute to a gloomy forecast for global economic recovery and political stability. In this background, it becomes necessary for India, China, and the US to engage in periodic dialogues both at official and non-official levels. It is not inevitable that the interests of each of the three powers are at conflict, whether with respect to the extended neighbourhood of India or with regard to South East, and East Asia.

3

Main Elements of US Foreign Policy Towards Asia

B. Raman

(Given are the salient points of a presentation that I will be making at a seminar on '*Re-evaluating US Foreign Policy towards Asia*' being jointly organised at the University of Madras on January 09, 2012, by the Chennai Centre for China Studies, the Centre for Asia Studies, Chennai, and the Department of Politics and Public Administration, University of Madras)

As President Obama nears the end of his first term, and gets ready to seek a second term, he has sought to give a new focus to the US foreign policy towards Asia.

This new focus is marked by two characteristics. Firstly, an open and uninhibited expression of the US concerns over China's ever-increasing economic and military capabilities, and its far from transparent intentions. Secondly, an open expression of the US determination to maintain and strengthen its capabilities in the Asia-Pacific region in order to safeguard its strategic interests, but also other like-minded countries—Japan, South Korea, Australia, the Philippines, Vietnam, India—which share the US concerns over China's capabilities and intentions.

While the first three years of Obama's first term were marked by preoccupation with the threats emanating to the security of the US Homeland from the Af-Pak region, and from the global terrorists operating from that region, the coming years of the Obama Presidency will be marked by a new preoccupation with likely threats to the US economic, commercial, and other strategic interests from the increasing capabilities and intentions of China and to the critical infrastructure—civilian as well as military—in the US Homeland from the well-concealed Chinese cyber war capabilities.

The US does not anticipate a conventional war with China, but it does fear a major threat from China to its naval primacy in the Pacific and the

Indian Ocean regions, and to its commercial interests in the region marked by the passage of nearly US$ 1.2 trillion of its foreign trade every year through the South China Sea. The US also fears a major threat to its critical infrastructure in the US Homeland as well as overseas from the Chinese cyber war capabilities.

The US nervousness is increased by the fact that while considerable information is available on China's modernisation and expansion of its conventional, nuclear and space-related capabilities, very little information is available on China's cyber war capabilities. Till recently, fears over likely threats to US nationals and interests from the attempts of Al Qaeda-led global terrorists to acquire weapons of mass destruction capabilities remained an important driving force of the US strategic doctrine. Since the beginning of last year, there are indications that fears over likely threats to the US critical infrastructure in times of peace, and war from China's cyber war capabilities, have become an important driving force of the US strategic doctrine relating to the Asia-Pacific region.

Since May last year, there have been reliable reports in sections of the US media about the examination of the outlines of a cyber war doctrine to meet the new needs of the expanding threat scenario. A significant element of the cyber war doctrine reportedly under contemplation is making explicit the US determination to use its military forces in response to a cyber attack if the gravity of the attack crosses a certain threshold. These reports of a cyber war doctrine under evolution and the recent decisions of the Obama Administration to maintain and strengthen its military capabilities in the Asia-Pacific region are meant to convey a carefully-disguised cautionary to China to behave itself not only in the high seas, but also in the cyber space. The US is determined to prevent China from acquiring an asymmetric advantage in cyber space by threatening China with a military response against targets in its territory to neutralise its cyber war capabilities should it become necessary.

The Pentagon's strategic defence guidance document titled 'Sustaining US Global Leadership: Priorities for 21st Century Defence' released at a press conference attended by Obama on January 05, 2012, says, "Over the long term, China's emergence as a regional power will have the potential to affect the US economy and our security in a variety of ways. Our two countries have a strong stake in peace and stability in East Asia and an interest in building a cooperative bilateral relationship. However, the growth of China's military power must be accompanied by greater clarity of its strategic intentions in order to avoid causing friction in the region. The US will continue to make the necessary investments to ensure that we maintain regional access and the ability to operate freely in keeping with our treaty obligations and with international law. Working closely with our network of allies and partners, we will continue to promote a rules-based international order that ensures underlying stability and encourages the peaceful rise of new powers, economic dynamism, and constructive defence cooperation."

The focus in the Pentagon document released to the media is on China's non-cyber capabilities, but there are reports that the US is equally concerned—if not more—over China's cyber warfare capabilities and intentions.

The US is still keen on strengthening a co-operative convergence with China to restore the health of the global economy, to deal with problems relating to climate and environment and to de-nuclearise Iran and North Korea. Nuclear non-proliferation will continue to be an important US foreign policy objective. For this, it needs China's co-operation. At the same time, there are growing concerns in Washington D.C. that the US' benign strategic intentions and objectives might not be matched by equally benign Chinese intentions and objectives. It would, therefore, be necessary to reinforce the US presence and capabilities in the Asia-Pacific region.

This objective is sought to be achieved by a unilateral revamp of the US presence and capabilities and through co-operation with other like-minded and equally concerned countries without giving an impression of an attempt to promote a new alliance to contain China. What the new Pentagon document talks of is not a new alliance, but a network of US allies and partners. Though not explicitly stated, the US obviously views Japan, South Korea, and Australia as allies in this network and India, Vietnam, the Philippines, and possibly other ASEAN countries as partners. These unilateral and multilateral efforts will be projected in the months to come not as an attempt to contain China, but as an exercise to bring China into the mainstream of Asian peace and security.

The US is interested in India playing an activist role in this new exercise for a network of allies and partners, but does India reciprocate this interest? The answer to this is not clear. India has already been playing an activist role in relation to its strategic co-operation with Myanmar, Vietnam, Japan, and South Korea. It has also been increasing its strategic co-operation with Singapore and Australia. Its relations with the US have improved in the fields of counter-terrorism and maritime security. But India is still inclined to view these relationships as without any linkages or networking which could trigger off alarm in Beijing.

India and the other Asian countries with which India has established a one-to-one strategic partnership, share the openly-expressed US concerns over China's capabilities, intentions and objectives but they are not prepared to say so openly. They would want to promote a policy of mutual consultations and assistance in security matters, but not in a manner that could alarm China.

India has its own unique concerns relating to China arising from the failure of the India-China border talks to make any progress and the growing strategic co-operation between China and Pakistan. It has to evolve its own strategy for dealing with China in a manner that would not make these two issues more complex and complicated than they are now. What would be in India's interest is not a networked relationship, but a mutually assisted and reinforced relationship on a one-to-one basis with a gradually expanding basket of issues that could promote a strategic convergence.

Two such issues in the Indo-US strategic basket relate to counter-terrorism and maritime security. The time has come to add cyber security not only against non-State actors, but also against common States of concern to this basket. China's undetermined cyber warfare capabilities could pose as much of a threat to India as they do to the US. The time has also come for the US and Indian Navies to think of a graduated surge in their navy-to-navy co-operation by way of training, joint exercises, exchanges of visits, intelligence liaison, etc. (January 08, 2012)

4

US Exploitation of Sino-Soviet Dispute to its Advantage

N. Narasimhan

Pre-emptions

I am grateful to the Chennai Centre for China Studies, Dept. of Politics and Public Administration, University of Madras, and the Centre for Asia Studies, Chennai for giving this opportunity to meet this distinguished group, under the pretense of sharing some thoughts on the theme of the Seminar, compelling one in the process to shed sloth and exert a bit to put down some lines.

Special word of thanks is owed to Prof. Suryanarayan and Dr. D.S. Rajan to have called me, despite my obvious lack of credentials in terms of scholarship, total absence of its 'sine qua non', publications to credit (or discredit!), and invisibility in seminar circuits. I wonder whether they need to be congratulated for their boldness, or commiserated for recklessness, in taking this gamble at High Noon.

The odds may be doubled by those who are aware that the little background I have is more Sino-centric, and the US Polity is not an area of normal specialisation for my ilk. But then anybody can pass off as an 'expert' on the US, as much as anyone can be an expert even on China these days.

Perspectives

The Seminar theme is being anchored on Henry Kissinger (Dr. K) and his latest publication 'On China' (KOC). This eases the way somewhat, as one had occasion to do a bit of digging into KOC recently; though my focus then was on the takeaways from it for the more proximate concern over the dire straits of the current status of India-China relations. So, straying into that area a bit this time too (paras 38-41) is no hangover. It reflects a strong belief that 'it is an ill-wind that blows India no good'.

In an appreciation of the unfolding drama of the US-China relations with the Soviet Union in a supporting role, KOC could be usefully supplemented with some of his earlier writings, both for details of how the domestic polity impinged on the US government's decision-making in this case, and how astutely they were managed by Dr. K, against difficult odds. There were serious policy and philosophical differences in the country on the macro perspective of Super power relations in a bi-polar world. There were also intra-USG Departmental sensitivities and infirmities which had scope to derail the rapprochement process, and therefore, necessitated the basics to be kept under the wraps till the optimal moment. They all constitute essential reference, besides providing immense cerebral entertainment, and should be seen as a whole.

In fact, his elaborate treatment of the developments within the USG preceding the momentous February 1972 statement announcing the Nixon visit, finalised by him and Chou-enlai, ('....will shake the world'), in his earlier book 'The White House Years' (WHY), has greater depth and detail. It provides many insights, which are not available in KOC for obvious reasons of differences in scope, objectives, and the additional space needed to record and analyse the events of the subsequent four decades.

It occurs that Dr. K would not have been very comfortable, outwardly at least, with the prescribed title formulation of the Paper, for the phrase 'US Exploitation'. He was at pain on record to upbraid as 'crude' the even milder phrase, 'Use' of China against the Soviet Union, employed by the State Dept., then dominated by the Sovietologists, while seeking to warn Nixon of the dire consequences to US-Soviet Union relations and for the world peace, with little compensating advantage.

His alternate formulations, for the motivation and rationale for the ongoing efforts by the US to open up to China, were couched mellifluously in these terms. "... We wanted to create an incentive for both to improve their relations with us ... Our objective was to purge our foreign policy of all sentimentality... We moved towards China... to shape a global equilibrium...

for constructive ends - to give each Communist power a stake in better relation with us..."

This is more than semantic sophistry as we can see in greater detail to time permitted extent.

An Obiter: It is necessary that India's 'strartegy' over the decades, how it had fared, evaluated and recalibrated in all our important external relations, gets articulated in similar fashion for edification of the nation , and to get the best results, commensurate with its potential.

The 'Dispute'

The second part of the formulation, 'Sino-Soviet dispute', also admits of a useful digression to obtain a realistic perspective. Over the decades, this broad description of the complicated gamut of Sino-Soviet relations had comprised diverse elements with varying interpretations, claims, nuances, ranging over the spectrum of 'Ideology', itself with standalone components—purity of Marxist-Leninist Philosophy, World Revolution Strategies, Leadership Tactics, Real-/Geo-Politics, Clash of Cultures, Personalities of Titans.

China and the Soviet Union employed numerous strategems, not excluding forays into war/brink of war situations, to further their respective, competing/conflicting national interests and ambitions, using nuanced mixes of these ingredients to shield their real goals at a given point of time, which got conveniently dubbed with the label, the 'Sino-Soviet Dispute'.

This umbrella also spawned lesser, localised sub-texts authored by the likes of Tito, Ho Chiminh, Kim Il Sung, Castro et al, to suit their own specific game plays and exploit those of the two Biggies.

Dr. K has fascinatingly, and in engaging detail traced the wide sweep and violent swings in the relations between the Soviet Union and China over the past sixty years with acceptable acumen, if not impeccable impartiality all the time, bringing out the fact that these had never been at any level of comfort to either of them, vitiated, 'ab initio', by historic developments from Czarist, Chinese Imperial eras, feeding into mutual suspicion and distrust-- from the Chinese side, huge, long-nursed grievances of territorial occupation of its territories, economic exploitation, and, later, fears of an imposition of US-Soviet condominium over the world, with potential to set at naught China's own dreams and visions of its future as a world power matching all its past Imperial glory. These are peppered with riveting quotes of the leading dramatis personae, culled from documents become available more recently.

The Pacific Duo—Duel and Duet

Nixon was not the first President to 'discover' the efficacy of normalising US-China relations. Even at the birth of People's Republic of China in 1949, before (neutral) rational policymaking in the US was swept away by the domestic tide of the 'Who lost China' debate, and the Korean war precipitated by the machinations of Kim Il Sung, entangling the trio, People's Republic of China-United States-Soviet Union (PRC-US-SU), apparently unwittingly despite their better judgments, and the accompanied advent of virulent anti China/anti Communist sentiment in the country, statesmen like Dean Acheson had contemplated developing relations with the new regime in Peking.

JFK and a succession of Presidents/Presidential aspirants had noted, usually through the medium of an article in the Foreign Affairs or an important address to a suitable forum, meant to set out the policy framework of the new/incoming Administration, the desirability of developing relations with China, mainly on grounds that it was too big to be ignored/isolated. But they were always compelled to attach, out of prevailing domestic considerations, riders/conditionalities like that China had to become mainstream, abjure its revolutionary stance and activities. These sentiments were however too generalised, and in passing, that scope to discuss strategies like leveraging the triangular relations with the Soviet Union did not figure in the avowals of that time.

At one point Dr. K himself notes, with uncharacteristic self effacement, that it was inevitable that China and the US would find a way to come together, given the necessities of time. It would have happened sooner or later, whatever the leadership of either country. Both nations were exhausted from war (Vietnam for the US and border clashes with the Soviet Union for China). The Moscow menace took their minds off the confrontations in Vietnam and Taiwan and quelled even ritual denunciations. Nixon's contribution was his decisiveness ('going for the jugular') and his immunity from serious attack of 'sell out' from the domestic Right

Dr.K's broad segmentation of the evolution of US-PRC relations into three major, distinct phases, from the perspective of the dominant underlying current governing each, is over all accepted by cognoscenti. The first is the two 'frozen' decades (1949-69) of open hostility, marked by an actual war in Korea and near war situations twice in the Taiwan straits. The second phase (1969-89) can be justifiably termed as the Kissinger Act/Show, in view of his titular role, when relations were normalized with a dramatic oeuvre, shrouded in tantalising secrecy, and progressed under dominating , yet contrasting, leadership of Mao and Deng from the Chinese side. The third chapter (1989-2009) is the period of 'refreeze' in the relations when 'human rights' constituted the major sticking point, post Tien Anmen massacre, impeding the linear progression of the previous two decades.

Fair to say empirically that the so-called 'Sino-Soviet Dispute' had been a factor, one way or the other, in this denouement only in the first two stages. The symbolic beginning of the disintegration of the Soviet bloc, from that of the Berlin Wall in 1989, culminating in the dissolution of the Soviet Union itself in 1993, literally marked the closure of the 'Dispute'. The corresponding rise of China in the last phase moved the bilateral relations between the US and China to a different, totally new, and currently much-debated level.

Need to keep in view that not only in DR. K's account, but in most other studies of the evolution of the global geo-political developments in this period, we largely depend on research and writings of scholars/historians of Western origin, intellectual discipline and orientation, even where they quote Chinese and Soviet documents and sources. Despite this limitation, it can be safely postulated that the seed for the US-China rapprochement had already started sprouting with the determination of the Chinese, 'to sup with the devil, if China's interests warranted it'—a signal Chairman Mao sent quite early in the 1960s through a non-governmental, old American friend (Edgar Snow), which got lost in the cacophony of current crisis of the day in the US.

Even then, this decision was painfully arrived at, compellingly by the tremendous heat of unrelenting Soviet pressure on China. The bloody hostilities which broke out at the two extremities of their borders in Ussuri and Xinjiang in the spring and autumn of 1969, following a succession of earlier crises, precipitated the decision to cross the Rubicon of opening to the US from the Chinese side, at the time it did. It was preceded by considerable internal debate and soul-searching, including high-powered strategic deliberations by four veteran Marshals of the People's Liberation Army (PLA) Long March vintage, called back from Great Proletarian Cultural Revolution (GPCR) disgrace.

The Triangle In Motion (TIM)—Some Analysis

In this highly intricate, tripodal minuet, China seems to have been the smartest/nimblest, in time and again exploiting the susceptibilities of the other two to its immense advantage. All along, in every crisis situation, the Chinese were considerably the weaker of the three, but managed to come up trumps, through manipulations of all genre, taking maximum advantage of the circumstances prevailing, to their overall benefit; even if in the short-term, or on any particular occasion, they might have suffered a temporary setback, as in the case of their adventure to teach Vietnam a lesson following the Cambodian invasion crisis (1979), or paid a heavy price in terms of humungous domestic privations (many times unrelated to foreign policy, except in point of time).

Mao calculated, correctly as it turned out most of the time, that neither Super power would permit his defeat by the other—a consummate practice of the Zhuge Liang Empty Theatre Strategem, turning material weakness into psychological asset.

It is now quite clear, in the light of the significant disclosures from even Chinese sources, besides the unraveling of the Soviet era documents that the real strategic contest was between the Soviet Union and China to ensure that the US was not used by the other to its own detriment. It seemed rarely the case of the US going any extraordinary length, or jeopardise its vitals, to outmaneuver either of the other two Communist countries, to achieve the best in a crisis.

For the US, it has been relatively a case of picking low hanging fruits. The Soviets, it appeared, were made to do all the huffing and puffing. The Chinese give the impression of agonising deep and long to extract the maximum benefits, while seeking to keep up the pretence, may be quite successfully with the domestic audience, of winning the game of 'Barbarian Management', in the best convoluted Confucian, Sun Tzu-ian (verbal) traditions.

At least in hindsight, being the weakest of the three, the situation was the direst, most of the time, for China leadership. Hence, the criticism of the 'Kissinger -Nixon' duo by their American domestic detractors that they should have extracted better terms from China for getting into a 'quasi-alliance', especially on the main, bilateral bone of contention, Taiwan, which could have spared the US considerable future problems, may not be far off the mark.

Again in retrospect, on the two major planks of compulsions constituting the US motivation/actions in the three way tussle, namely, the easing out of the Vietnam War and success in the negotiations underway for achieving US-Soviet détente, the trajectory of US moves was already independently well on course to success, and it was reasonable to suggest that the rapprochement with China was not critical in the eventual outcome of the two US goals.

Similarly, the impact of the US-China rapprochement on the eventual demise of the Soviet Union was marginal, if at all. The over-all Soviet decline was attributable substantially to other factors more intrinsic to Soviet polity, economy, its own missteps and miscalculations, without too significant external contributions by either the US or China.

An entirely Soviet/Russian centric study of the history of this era may possibly bring out different shades of perspectives and conclusions. But it is inescapable that the extant literature shows the Soviet Union coming a poor third in every one of these contests, in spite of its strong points on most metrics, especially in comparison to China.

It is not that Dr. K's accounts alone, undoubtedly Sino centric, if not that of a Sinophile as alleged by his harsh critics, lead to this impression. Unbiased, objective assessment also seem to point in this direction, even if one may overlook the caricature aspect of some of the reactions and statements attributed to Soviet leaders in these pages of KOC—like meeting of Mao with Khrushchev in Beijing in 1959. It is pertinent to note that KOC is clearly the result of extensive research into a wide range of all available up-to-date literature on the topics dealt with, including Soviet origin documents, besides many Chinese originals.

One essential point to be gleaned additionally from the relevant pages in the WHY is that the Soviet Union, (the overall impression of a bumbling super power Inspector Clouseau, played for a sucker notwithstanding), was all along alive to the general trend of the ongoing US-China rapprochement, even though possibly not about all the specific steps and their timing,. It exerted fully, often, and at different levels, to warn the US about the serious consequences of any missteps it may take at the expense of the Soviet Union, to the overall Super power relationship in which, inter alia, serious negotiations for management of the threat and potential of nuclear war were afoot.

In response, Dr. K seemed to have tried not to mislead the Soviet Union by denial or evasion. He led them in on the basics to this extent:

- We do not accept the proposition that permanent hostility is the iron law of US-China relations
- Our policy is not aimed against the USSR
- We take no sides in the Sino-Soviet dispute

Chairman Mao's Role

From the vantage point of an observer outside the US-Soviet Union-China triangle, in retrospect, it is really breath taking how a couple of major lines of strategy employed by Chairman Mao had proved so effective and successful, for so long and so often. It, therefore, merits special highlighting, even if only sketchily.

One is the popularly called China's tactics of 'nuclear blackmail'—the 'put-on' nonchalance to the consequences of a nuclear war, first enunciated by Mao , in a seemingly innocuous way , in an insignificant meeting with the first Finnish Ambassador to China, on January 28, 1955, then developed into an 'ideology' at the Moscow Conference of Communist Parties in 1957, and later a sophisticated geo-political strategy, and successfully employed repeatedly, with great seriousness and finesse, in a variety of formulations and bilateral high level talks, wherein the other two powers hesitated to call the bluff. The Soviet Union emerged the more gullible of the two super powers in these episodes.

Like elsewhere, Mao had to pay a heavy price for this high stake game, like suffering suspension of Soviet nuclear and technical cooperation, cancellation aid projects, withdrawal of Soviet technicians, etc. (1958-60).

There was one American riposte, in March 1955, during the first Taiwan straits crisis, which proved the efficacy of Mao's nuclear blackmail by exception, when President Eisenhower and Secretary Dulles made a counter-nuclear threat to China expressing the US readiness to use tactical nuclear weapons. They had no intention to test Mao's grandiose claims of endurance in a nuclear war. They were merely showing readiness to defend the US national interest. Correspondingly, Mao showed that he was only willing at that time to announce China's imperviousness to nucler war, but was not ready to practice it.

Another 'totem' brandished by Chairman Mao was the concept of different versions of 'Revolution'—'Continuous', 'World', etc.—that segmented into First, Second, and Third. Mostly, it was used as a weapon against the Soviet Union in the guise of ideological purity, calling on all the countries and peoples to unite and fight against 'Imperialists', 'Reactionaries', 'Revisionists', 'Expansionists', 'Hegemonists' etc., It was as much a geopolitical tool for China against the US, as to isolate the Soviet Union, and counter the Soviet strategy enunciated through Brezhnev Doctrine, theory of Limited Sovereignty, and so on, in their duel/competition for world leadership in the anti-Imperialist struggle phase through its own counter interpretations of 'Peaceful Co-existence', 'World Peace', 'Nuclear Hegemony' , tailored adroitly to each specific crisis, as suited to its convenience and circumstances.

Dr. K credits Mao with making the best of the gameplay by being a contrarian. As against conventional diplomacy, where statesmen serve their objectives by bringing about confluence of interests, Mao did the opposite and learned to exploit overlapping hostilities. For example, Moscow-

Washington Conflict, which was the strategic essence of the cold war period; playing on the mutual hostilities of the nuclear super powers and using the tactic of nuclear black mail—the impression of being impervious to nuclear devastations. By these, he managed to bring about a kind of diplomatic sanctuary for China. Far from seeking the support of either super power as traditional balance of power theory would have counselled, he exploited the US-Soviet fear of each other by challenging each of the rivals simultaneously.

Parting Thoughts

Proportionate to the guidance it can provide for the future, History is useful for the policy makers and practitioners of Inter-State relations management. The general principles of Otto van Bismarck (and Sun Tzu?) about a country joining sides with the (numerically) stronger grouping in a pentangular-triangular relationship, as elaborated by Dr. K in this retelling of the TIM, offers plenty of scope to ponder. The cardinal issue is the difficulty in nuancing it further in ground reality situations, to determine joining which one of the other two will constitute the stronger grouping in the three-some at a given point of time . Be alert always to make nimble movements as warranted; nothing to be left ironclad or set in concrete.

In the many triangular relations of the future, India's focus may have to be on the following three involving itself — (i) India-China-US, (ii) India-China-Pak, and (iii) India-US-Pak. Obviously, the three sides comprising each of the three triangles do not stand apart unconnected in isolation but have points of intersection 'permutating' among all the three.

While it will be difficult to predict the intricacies of the dynamics of their evolution, one basic point is that no relationship is ever smooth and irritant free, that even the China-Pak bilateral relationship is not immutably bilateral and linear, sans twists and turns, and there are enough gaps between the lips and the teeth in any 'friendship', to watch out for by the smart, to play along.

Imperative to remind oneself constantly—relations between great powers can not be sustained by Inertia, Commerce or mere sentiment. Reciprocity has to be the bedrock. In particular, where China is concerned,

'Insistent posture' is the answer to the 'singularity' of their civilisationally rooted 'exceptionalist' diplomacy and (negotiating) tactics, hailed by Dr. K, who also clues in on the antidote.

5

US-China Relations: From Comprehensive Engagement to Hedging and Balancing

K.P. Vijayalakshmi

The 21st century has begun to witness Asia once again becoming the epicenter of global geopolitical activity. The US has a major role to play in this ongoing geopolitical shift. As the world's pre-eminent power, the US' influence is felt throughout the globe. Asia is no exception. However, with Asia leading the global recovery in the aftermath of the financial crisis of 2008, a CNN business blog posted by CNN Asia Business Analyst, Ramy Inocencio stated:

> *"Time may be running out much faster than we thought for the US. In just five years, China may lay claim to the title 'World's Largest Economy'. This is not coming from China fear mongers or doomsayers – this is according to the International Monetary Fund and its new GDP forecasts. The numbers: China's gross domestic product will rocket $8 trillion in the next five years to $19 trillion. The US GDP will grow $3.5 trillion in the same timeframe to $18.8 trillion. And it will be in that year - 2016 - that China's slice of world output will start to edge past the US': 18% versus 17.7%. In the years after, that gap is forecast to widen."*

In advanced economies (the US, Western Europe, and Japan), the pace of recovery has been held back by high unemployment rates, weak household balance sheets, and anaemic bank credit, and remains heavily dependent on macroeconomic policy support. In Asia, Gross Domestic Product (GDP) trend growth has exceeded that of the advanced economies over the last three decades, but this is the first time that the contribution of Asia—especially China—to global recovery has outstripped that of other regions. As the International Monetary Fund (IMF) forecast stated, "In China, the growth is expected to return to double digits in 2010, with private domestic demand boosted by measures to increase consumption and private investment. This is having positive spill overs for the rest of the region, as Chinese demand boosts imports, particularly of commodities and capital goods." China was not leading the recovery; it was also helping others in the region.

Business estimates too painted a similar picture: Goldman Sachs' first Brazil, Russia, India, China and South Africa (BRIC) projections a decade ago suggested that China would overtake the US total GDP by 2042. At the time many thought the projections were optimistic; in retrospect, perhaps the estimates were more conservative. Taking the growth experience of the 2000 into consideration, China is now expected to catch up to the US in the late 2020s; if the sustained impact of the global crisis (the debt crisis in the G-7 nations) is included, this development may occur in the early 2020s. (Steinbock, 2010). Frederic Neumann, Managing Director of Asian Economics Research, the Hong Kong and Shanghai Banking Corporation, Hong Kong, confirmed that while Purchasing Power Parity (PPP) is one credible way to measure GDP, there are other credible ways that show that China's path to economic #1 is much longer than the IMF's forecast expects. For him, "US dollar terms are a different way to measure China growth. Using this, 'it would take much longer for the Chinese economy to overtake the US—probably 2025'. And while PPP measures domestic purchasing power, US dollars are a better gauge for purchasing power on the world stage." Clearly, while the debate continues, it seems more about 'when' not 'if' China will be the world's biggest economy. It also means that China along with Asia will be influencing strategic developments in the world.

Interestingly, in an Annual Strategy Conference held by US Army College in April 2012 titled 'The Future of US Grand Strategy in an Age of Austerity: Challenges and Opportunities', there was broad agreement among experts that sustaining US engagement in East Asia was especially important due to the rising power of China (along with issues such as North Korea's threatening behaviour, and the potential for further nuclear weapons proliferation in the region).

The US seems to be fully aware that Asia's development, and within it China's rise, is too powerful to be overlooked; therefore, it has outlined a policy that 'pivots' towards Asia, or more accurately has stated that it is in the process of 'rebalancing' its Asia policy which would include China. The term 're-balancing', according to latest reports, encompasses two separate processes—the US military is rebalancing its global assets from other regions to Asia, as well as rebalancing within the Asia-Pacific region, reducing the concentration of forces from northeast Asia to a more widely distributed focus throughout the entire region

In fact, as Washington announced its 'rebalancing' policy in early 2012, and the Pentagon announced in June that it would station 60 per cent of its navy in the Pacific by 2020, it drew responses from the countries in the region including China and US allies around the world. Worried over the larger strategic importance of the US 'pivot' or rebalancing in Asia, many raised the following questions: whether this would lead to conflict or cooperation between US and China? Further, what is the substance of the pivot? Secondly, to what extent is this new and what are the various aspects of it? Finally, what are some of the concerns about it? Recent response from China on this matter provided a fresh set of questions: is there now a Chinese 'pivot' strategy to counter the US? What are the main features of such a policy? What would be its impact on the region and on the strategic interests of the US and India? Answers to these questions will need deeper analysis that is probably only beginning, however, at issue is the need to establish the drivers and trends of US policy towards China.

It is now widely accepted that China represents the most important bilateral relationship for the US, yet US' China policy has generated constant controversy. The Sino-American relationship has always had to balance diverse policy interests such as containment of USSR in the Cold War, security in East Asia, including the Taiwan question, trade and commercial relations, arms proliferation, and human rights. In the US, the battle for policy formulation included on the one hand, executive-branch actors such as the National Security Council (NSC) State Department, Commerce Department, the White House, and the National Economic Council (NEC) and political actors, such as the US Congress and powerful lobbying groups on the other, each having a stake in policymaking.

The complex interaction between these players has at times constrained policy actions and outcomes. Further, it has produced different sets of foreign policy assumptions and goals under different administrations. For instance, China continues to be tested on the assumption of whether economic openness leads to political liberalisation with the one-party rule that appears durable for the near future. The other test has been on whether having staked its claim for a rising stardom based on its ability to deliver continued growth and stability, can China balance its economic growth and expansion with a growing role in international affairs? For the US, the question remains whether China will act as a 'responsible stakeholder' in the international system or be a 'strategic competitor'?

It is in this context, this paper argues that a brief assessment of the US-China Relations from the era of normalisation, that is, the seventies to the twenty first century is necessary to understand the basic motivations of the US' China policy. Secondly, it argues that the shifting American interests over time have altered the foreign policy orientation of the US towards China as different administrations balanced American global strategy posture with compulsions of a regional and bilateral nature. Thirdly, it is contended that the US economic engagement with China has expanded as result of the consensus created by supporters in the executive branch that countries that are deeply connected by trade and other commercial interests do not go to war. Not only that, economic ties would foster the development of a free market economy in China. Free market capitalism would lead to eventual democratisation that would negate the assumption of conflict between the two.

However, the paper also suggests that these assumptions are frequently taken negatively by various influential groups that then create turbulence in policy. When these groups have combined with changes in presidency, US-China relations have been plagued by serious problems despite growth in trade. This school views as apparent that a huge trade imbalance (or deficit for the US of US$ 162 billion in 2004 and over US$ 200 billion in 2005) should be the focus as the value of trade itself. Clearly the deficit has sparked new and quite virulent protectionist sentiments and anti-China feelings in America. The paper also contends the prevalence of elements of realist thinking in the US government, which claim that a contest for supremacy between China and the US is inevitable, and perhaps already under way. In this perspective, appeals for US-Chinese cooperation appear outmoded, naive, and temporary. The goal of this paper is to contribute to the current policy debate on 'Re-evaluating America's foreign policy towards Asia' by focussing on US-China relations from Nixon to Obama.

In main, the determinants of US policy included partisan politics, bureaucratic wrangling and ideological preferences of presidency. Hence this paper argues that the domestic debates and internal process of policy formulation are significant markers that shape policy. It is also contended that there is both hostility and support for a policy of engagement towards China from both Democrats and Republicans. It is argued that in the case of China, the policy formulation process combined with the Presidency's preferences reflects the efforts to build consensus for policy options that help to balance internal, domestic, and international goals of the US foreign policy.#

The US-China Relations: An Overview
Between 1971 and 1972, President Richard Nixon and Chairman Mao Zedong re-established diplomatic contact, not because American and Communist ideologies had suddenly become more compatible, but because of their respective geopolitical necessities. The relationship between the US and China established by Nixon, Kissinger and their successors in the Carter and Regan administrations was, in many ways the strangest, most extraordinary relationship America has had with any nation. China was not just any other country to the US, and the relationship that the US worked out with China's Communist Party leadership has been based on the unstated premise that China is unique. In the midst of America's ideological struggle against the

---

\#   For a general discussion of how domestic political factors shape foreign policy, see Eugene R. Wittkopf and James M. McCormick (eds.), *The Domestic Sources of American Foreign Policy*. For a discussion of domestic determinants of China Policy, see Robert Sutter, The China Quandary, *Domestic Determinants of US China Policy, 1972-82.*

Soviet Union, the US formed a close partnership with China, a country whose leadership was no less dedicated to Leninist political principles than the leaders of Moscow. China was America's partner in fighting the Cold War; Washington proceeded to support, arm, share intelligence with and nurture the economy of a Chinese government it had previously attempted to overthrow. For America's policymaking elite, relationship with China was considered to be special and the need was for continual engagement with it (Kissinger, 2001).

However, the US-China relationship was also beset with contradictions as early National Security Council document NSSM 124: Next steps towards the People's Republic of China (PRC) dated April 19, 1971 shows, "Our (US) longer term objectives should be to draw the PRC into serious discussion of the problems involved not only in our bilateral relationship but also in a more general relaxation of tensions in East Asia." and, "Our objectives should be to move US-PRC contacts onto a governmental plane as rapidly as possible."

Several other documents show that during the Cold War, both sides were determined to counter the influence of the Soviet Union. Subsequently, however, there was a shift in the US policy. It seemed to switch from a Cold War strategy of using China to blunt Soviet expansion to one of engaging China for business. Towards this end, the US opened its markets to Chinese goods, encouraged American firms to invest in China, and granted them the Most-Favoored-Nation (MFN) status, thus, laying the groundwork for building economic ties that were broader in scope than with any other communist country. Ostensibly, the purpose for this move was because the policymakers and domestic interest groups assumed that economic dependence on the American export market would lead to more humane governance in China. This marked a significant shift in the American perception that now looked at China differently and Sino-US relations more bilaterally. It was argued that good US-China relations would be beneficial not only for mutual commercial benefits, but also help to bring about a change in the Chinese government attitude towards Human Rights issues.

The US-China Relations Between 1969-89: A Brief Account

In the American perception, China, in its long history, had rarely chosen to experience dealing with other societies on the basis of equality. As Kissinger points out, for the greatest part, it was dominant in its region; in the 19th century and the first half of the twentieth; it was humiliated by the imperial powers. Before that, it had felt most comfortable when it was able to stand aloof and self-contained—as a culture whose uniqueness placed it beyond the reach of outsiders—and, until approximately the 1500s, as the most advanced nation in science and technology. For China, there was nothing unnatural about living apart from the US. What brought the two nations together was their leaders' awareness of a common threat. The Chinese leaders saw the buildup of Soviet military power along their border, including nuclear missiles and forty modern combat divisions over a million men. By 1969, it was obvious to China that Marxist theory not only did not shield it from Soviet military pressures but provided a pretext for them. For the newly promulgated Brezhnev Doctrine claimed for the Kremlin the special right to use military power within the Communist world to enforce its unity. For the US, opportunity was merging with necessity. Under the impact of the Vietnam War, the US foresaw and recognised the role China might play in establishing a new Asian balance of power. (Kissinger, 2001)

Historically, it may be recalled that the innovative policies towards China and the Soviet Union were at the heart of the Nixon-Kissinger 'grand design' for world politics. Nixon and Kissinger sought to manipulate international relations so as to achieve very traditional goals of the US foreign policy; they cited, for instance preserving a central role for American power in world politics and thwarting hostile political configurations abroad that could 'isolate' and potentially endanger American society as primary reason for American investment; this was apparent in their so-called 'China Strategy'. A recent publication titled *'The Kissinger Transcripts: The Top Secret Talks with Beijing and Moscow'* revealed that the American assumption was that the weakening of the Chinese economy as a result of Mao's experiments and the Cultural Revolution had made China no longer a precariously threatening model of social development to be isolated from international forums and the western commercial system. Nixon believed that it was time for Washington to seek an opening with Beijing and even to warn the Soviets against threatening China because of the Sino-Soviet border clashes that took place during the year 1969. Further, Nixon believed that rapprochement with China was necessary so as to prevent Asian countries from worrying about US-Soviet 'cabal against the Chinese' because of the US-Soviet détente. Furthermore, he also feared that if Moscow grew stronger it could influence China in the sense of controlling its policies and action. Therefore, Nixon believed that it was essential to uphold China's territorial integrity so that it remained an independent power free from foreign control. (Burr, 1999)

In geopolitical terms, there were powerful reasons for a rapprochement with China to balance the Soviet Union. Nixon and Kissinger worked on improving ties with the People's Republic of China knowing the fact that China would engage with the US to use it as a counter balance against the Soviet in spite of Beijing's rhetorical hostility towards American policy. In addition, the perception was that the US-PRC relations would make the Soviet very nervous which might compel it to improve ties with the US. In the assessment of veteran US China expert, Kissinger, new links between China and the US flourished so long as the two sides were in a position to concentrate on the common objective of resisting what their communiqués came to describe as 'hegemony'; which meant resisting Soviet attempts to upset the global or Asian balance of power and some tacit agreement on an appropriate strategy to achieve this end. (Kissinger, 2001). What led to the breakthrough in a relationship that had basically been foundering on mere expressions of a desire for a dialogue was the fact that both sides sought progress.

Under Nixon, the policy making was subjected to a great degree of centralisation with his hierarchical and closed advisory system. Henry Kissinger, to all purposes his right-hand man, handled policymaking through a series of back-channel contacts that circumvented the State Department and held policy initiatives tightly within the White House (Garrison, 2005). Thus despite the Taiwan lobby, there does not seem to be any major setback to his policy initiatives. Further, Nixon overcame the policy constraints that could have been the result of Congressional debates on abandoning Taiwan by situating the China discourse within the overall foreign policy context rather than a bilateral one. Crucially, his China policy was successful because the Chinese responded to his overtures at the highest level, unlike the Johnson period (Goh, 2005). As Kissinger recalled, China was willing to consider talks outside the Warsaw channels at the ambassadorial leveler through other channels 'to reduce tensions between China and the US and fundamentally improve relations'. It did not make such talks conditional on the settlement of the Taiwan issue (Kissinger 2011, p. 223). In Kissinger's own estimation, the problem of bilateral negotiations was not only made difficult by twenty years of isolation, cultural differences between American and Chinese approaches to negotiations, but also due to the differences between Nixon and his own diplomats. For Kissinger, Nixon and he saw this occasion not so much to remove irritants as to conduct geopolitical dialogue. (Ibid., p. 225.)

President Gerald Ford seemingly shared the strategic calculus that had motivated the Nixon administration to open relations with China. To him, the US policy towards China was a critical part of the administration's effort to offset American setbacks in Asia. However, the Ford Administration was not prepared to normalise relations. The domestic political cost was too high for a president looking to be elected as there was mounting conservative criticism within the Republican Party on the policy of détente with the Chinese at the cost of Taiwan. Thus, he sought the benefit of improved relations without paying the price of normalisation on China's terms. The Chinese too were insistent on normalisation despite presidential elections as their international status had improved and they recognised the US' perception of the enhanced strategic importance of China. However, despite domestic politics, Kissinger sought intermediary agreements with the Chinese that would caution the Soviets and curb its 'adventurism' (Ross, 1995 p. 72 ff). In fact, Kissinger argues that Deng unlike Mao assumed an identity of strategic interests with the US and concentrated on achieving a parallel implementation. Deng, according to Kissinger, changed the Chinese position toward the Soviet Union from containment to explicit strategic hostility. (Kissinger, 2011, p. 348-349.)

Exhaustive accounts of this period show that when the Carter administration entered office the US and China had already gone a long way towards reaching agreement on normalisation. However, normalisation though high on the agenda of President Carter, suffered from the American proposal on Taiwan. As Secretary Vance stated in his memoirs, the US was intent on pushing for a maximalist position on Taiwan, which it did not expect the Chinese to accept. In fact, Vance even felt that this position may have to be abandoned as Deng would reject it.

However, as President Carter and Secretary of State Cyrus Vance began pursuing US-Soviet détente, the Chinese had begun to get restive over the policy of waiting and the shifting nature of American goals with China. As records show, the Chinese leadership, especially Deng was eager to proceed on normalisation in order to enlist Washington in a coalition to oppose and halt Soviet advances in the globe.

The Chinese were objecting to the shift in American strategic perspective under Carter that had an optimistic security outlook vis-a-vis the Soviets, (this was in reference to the US policy in the Middle East and the situation developing in Indochina) while they believed that the threat was increasing and the deference of normalisation that left them without strategic benefits (Kissinger, 2011, pp. 350-556). It was only by 1978, that the US and China developed a common threat perception of the Soviet Union and with both sides agreeing that the threat was significantly growing (Brzezenski, 1985).

Thus on December 15, 1978, the US and China announced in a joint communiqué that they agreed to normalise diplomatic relations from January 01, 1979. As the then Assistant Secretary for East Asian and Pacific Affairs Richard Holbrooke recalled '...establishing full diplomatic relations between China and the US. Without this action, announced on December 15, 1978, US-China relations could not have moved beyond a small, high-level connection with a limited agenda'.

Holbrooke also revealed how in order to reach this agreement, both sides had to make significant compromises on their long-standing positions on US-Taiwan relations. Describing how the famed Taiwan lobby, one of the most powerful in the US, still dominant in the conservative wing of American politics, was led by America's 'Mr. Conservative', Senator Barry

Goldwater, and the leading contender for the 1980 Republican nomination, Ronald Reagan, he further pointed out that the administration had to fight for normalisation all the way. In fact, Holbrooke emphasised that while Senator Goldwater took the US government to the Supreme Court to challenge, unsuccessfully, Carter's action; Ronald Reagan, in the 1980 presidential campaign, pledged partially to undo normalisation, only to abandon that position after he was elected.

Interestingly, the need to report and explain to the Congress any China-US agreement, made the Carter administration insist that normalisation negotiations will explicitly indicate US intentions to sell arms to Taiwan. Again, such expectations were shared by several members of the Congress who insisted that the any administration would need to be careful about giving the impression that the US would abandon its allies for a global strategic posture. In particular, Carter's National security Advisor, Zbigniew Brzezinski was seen as mainly concerned about challenging the Soviets on every front—politically, militarily, culturally, economically. He prevailed on the administration to push on some rightist regimes on human rights, but he also cut back US positions (in Brazil, Iran) to buttress strategic interests. His antagonist was Vance; and, more fitfully, Vice-President Mondale. As recalled by him in his memoirs, even while Vance was negotiating the SALT II agreements, he was pushing the MX missile, which basically violated the spirit of SALT, and the China 'card'. Brzezinski states that he enjoyed the startled look on Soviet Ambassador Dobrynin's face when he heard that full-scale diplomatic relations with China were in the offing than even his trip to China (Brzezinski, 1985). Carter's China policy seemed more a Brzezinski led one than by Secretary Vance as Carter overruled Vance and agreed that normalisation process should be expedited. These fights reflected deep ideological divides that had the potential to weaken the president. According to a study on presidential advisory system, "Carter's system, which placed him in the centre of a spokes-in-the-wheel advisory structure, for example, fostered competition rather than collegial relations because of the different interpretations of the Soviet threat between Secretary of State Cyrus Vance and National Security Adviser Zbigniew Brzezinski" (Garrisson, 2005).

Thus, Carter administration's bureaucratic infighting and political domestic considerations shaped the pace and conditionality of negotiations with China.

Normalisation of US-China relations had two major effects: one, it reduced the risk of Soviet military retaliation by minimising Beijing's isolation and second, it changed the Soviet perception that the US would be a mere spectator to Sino-Soviet hostilities. In addition, the US now recognised the Republic of China as part of the People's Republic of China. The assumption was that normalisation of relations could open the door to US-PRC strategic cooperation. The deteriorating relations between the Soviet Union and the US further consolidated the strategic imperative of selling military equipment to China. Unlike 1977, Carter by 1979 listened to Brzezinski's advice on liberalising restrictions on exports to China of technologies with potential military use. Deteriorating US Soviet relations had altered US China policy and arms sales of helicopters, high tech computers, etc. were considered. This would also enable rapid expansion of trade relations. It seemed that a stable course between the two was set, yet the election of President Reagan changed the situation.

The Chinese leaders were concerned about the Reagan Administration's intentions towards China. They feared that the President's ideological anti-communist sentiments and the influence of the Taiwan lobby in the administration would lead Washington to pursue a policy contrary to Chinese interests. Between 1981 and 1982, US-China relations experienced a reversal of the post 1969 trend of improving relations. Not only did the diplomatic relationship suffer amid threats and counter threats of down-graded relations, but military relations suffered as well. The reason for this was clear as China was holding the development of all aspects of US-China relations hostage to an agreement on Taiwan. An insider account by a former official of that time pointed out the President's tussle with the Department of State and his Secretary of State Haig over the Department's 'China Lobby' that was interested in US abandoning Taiwan. As Reagan himself recorded in his Diaries, "Press running wild with talk that I reversed myself on Taiwan because we're only selling them F-5E's and F-104's ... I think the China Lobby in the State Dept. is selling this line to appease the PRC, which doesn't want us to sell them [Taiwan] anything."

Reagan explained his decision, "The planes we're offering are better than anything the PRC has... Later on, if more sophistication is needed we'll upgrade and sell them F-5G's. Reagan argued that the 'Chinese will respect us more' if the US firmly rebuffed their Taiwan complaints" (Reagan Diaries 2007).

The joint communiqué of August 17, 1982, established a new set of rules governing both US and Chinese policies towards Taiwan. The US agreed to limit its arms sales to Taiwan and Beijing proclaimed its fundamental policy of peaceful unification.

The US policy under Reagan, to many observers, accommodated Chinese sensitivities on Taiwan by abiding with the existing agreements, yet the issue of selling fighters to Taiwan aided the Chinese perception that the US uses the 'Taiwan Card' to contain China and pursue its global strategy. Many critical Chinese essays emphasised that the US arms sales were a way of 'using Taiwan to contain China,' and assert that arms sales are a deliberately constructed obstacle to China's peaceful rise (Quingmin, 2006). However, in actual fact, the Reagan Administration deferred the decision on exporting the FX fighter to Taiwan when it provoked a crisis in China–US relations. "Taiwan's hopes were postponed from that time until the final key period of the 1992 US Presidential election, when incumbent G.H. Bush announced the selling of 150 F-16s to Taiwan." (Ibid.)

A legitimate question then arises as to why an anti communist ideologue like Reagan avoided crisis in US-China relations while George H.W. Bush an old friend of the Chinese, chose to do so? One school of thought in the US ascribes this to the problems and disagreements within State Department, and between the State and Defence Department. Declassified documentary evidence has revealed that when the US and China were negotiating the arms sales issue, Director of the Office of Policy Planning Paul Wolfowitz wrote two articles in 1981and 1982, criticising Haig's China policy. Many others in the Department also apparently believed that Haig overestimated the strategic value of the relationship with China. After Haig resigned and Shultz became the Secretary of State, Wolfowitz was appointed Assistant

Secretary for East Asian and Pacific Affairs, which marked a change in the level of importance accorded China in America's East Asia policy.

The basic conclusion that can be drawn is that relations between the US Congress and the administrative departments were already tenuous because of the Taiwan arms sales issue. The Department of State, Defence and the NSC were deep into the discussions on Taiwan arms sales with the need to promote strategic cooperation with China, but eventually the resignation of NSA Allen, a Taiwan supporter, weakened the White House determination to sell arms to Taiwan. Further, after the August 17 communiqué, China continued to press for the US concessions on a range of issues. The US, on the other hand shifted to a far less compliant posture. While it accommodated China sensitivity on Taiwan by scrupulously abiding by existing agreements it was quite forthcoming on trade and military issues only when it served US interest. On issues of conflict, the Reagan administration consistently adopted measures that bluntly signaled its firm resolves not to succumb to Chinese pressures. It must also be noted that on April 30, 1984, President Reagan witnessed the initialing of a cooperative agreement on nuclear energy. Secretary of Energy John Herrington signed the agreement on July 23, 1985. On July 24, 1985, President Reagan submitted to Congress the 'agreement between the US and the People's Republic of China Concerning Peaceful Uses of Nuclear Energy'. Again it was done despite Congressional Concerns.

The irony of the Reagan administration's China Policy was that for an American President most personally attached to Taiwan, and a president more suspicious of Beijing than any other President since Richard Nixon, his administration developed the most successful US policy towards the PRC since the original rapprochement between the two countries. Not only did Ronald Reagan's China policy serve the US interests in developing stable and cooperative relations at minimal costs to other US interests, he also developed bipartisan support for it.

Through the 1980s, Washington and Beijing never fully resolved many of the issues that had plagued relations since the first days of rapprochement. It was their statesmen who succeeded in developing policies that enabled the US and China to cooperate notwithstanding those differences. As Kissinger noted, in the end, "The Sino-American relationship in the 1980s was in transition from a Cold War pattern to a global international order that created new challenges for the US-China partnership" (Kissinger, 2011, p. 393).

The Reagan years, thus established that what brought the two together in 1972 was a common concern about a threat of Soviet aggression. While that still held true, the broadening of the relations were based on the commonality of world views and American contention that the future major unifying factor in the next decade could well be economic interdependence (Nixon, 1982, quoted in Kissinger, 2011)

The US-China Relations During the Presidency of George H.W. Bush

George H.W. Bush probably knew more about China and its issues in Chinese-American relations than any US president. In 1971, as an Ambassador to the UN, he had been assigned the hopeless task of leading the fight to keep a seat for Taiwan in the General Assembly. He spent the better part of two years in Beijing as head of the American liaison office in China in 1974 and 1975. After he occupied the White House in 1989, he perceived no need for initiatives on China policy from the Department of State or the National Security Council. He intended to be his own desk officer for Chinese affairs. When George H.W. Bush was inaugurated as President in January 1989, most of the clouds that had darkened the Chinese-American relationship in the early 1980s were gone. This time, the Chinese perceived a friend in the White House, the first American President to have served as his country's representative in China.

President Bush's vision of the Chinese-American relationship was closer to that of Nixon and Kissinger than to that of Shultz or Reagan. Unlike Shultz, he considered China to be an important strategic partner in the struggle against the Soviet Union. Unlike Reagan, the concerns of the people of Taiwan were not absolute on his agenda.

Bush was not unaware of problems that existed between China and the US. Some of the eminent ones were:

- Chinese arms sales to Middle East countries, especially the sale of anti-ship Silkworm missiles to Iran which posed a grave threat to US Navy vessels protecting shipping in the Persian Gulf

- There was also evidence that the Chinese were supplying missiles and nuclear technology to Pakistan and countries less friendly to Americans
- Accusations on the Chinese government for obstructing the import of American goods into China which frustrated American businessmen invested in joint Chinese- American ventures
- China's treatment of its own people and its persistent violation of the Universal Declaration of Human Rights

The furor that arose in the US during the Bush administration over the Tianamen Square incident in China brought the entire relationship to a standstill. Prior to the Tiananmen Square episode, US-China relations had relaxed to a point where the US removed some of its strategic controls on sales of weapons-related technology. The event that took place on June 04, 1989 in the Tiananmen Square compelled President Bush to suspend the sale of weapons to China and the US broke off contacts with the PLA. There were demands from candidate Clinton for stronger action to punish the 'Butchers of Beijing'. The Bush administration canceled a series of high-level visits. Under pressure from the Congress, the President ordered extensions on the visas of Chinese students in the US. President Bush announced that his administration would work to postpone Chinese applications for loans from international financial institutions. Congressional declarations from members across the political spectrum denounced the Chinese government and many legislators called for even harsher measures.

Chinese-American relations were probably the shakiest than they had been since Kissinger and Nixon reopened the dialogue with the People's Republic in the early 1970s. However, despite mounting public hostility towards China among the American people and Congressional pressures for punitive action, Bush and Scowcroft were determined to keep the lines of communication between Washington and Beijing open, in order to preserve some of the gains of the 1970s and 1980s. Still fighting the Cold War, they feared any harsh measures might drive the Chinese back into Soviet arms that will have huge national security implication. In December 1989, President George H.W. Bush sent his National Security Advisor, Brent Scowcroft and Deputy Secretary of State, Lawrence Eagleburger on a secret visit to Beijing to reassure the Chinese leaders as to the limited intentions of the US in their public diplomacy (Cohen, 2000). However, the 1990 visit of Jiang Zemin to the US helped to change the assumptions that shaped the relationship so far. Jiang Zemin's view was that relations between great nations were governed by national interest and not by projection of values across borders. He urged the US to work closely with the Chinese on a new international order that resembled the earlier Europeans' state system where domestic politics would be beyond the scope of foreign policy. The common ground that eventually came to be established highlighted Zemin's argument that ideological factors are not important to state relations especially as Cold War was receding.

President George H.W. Bush entered office with a well-formulated strategy toward China. The President, inclined towards a realpolitik perspective of great power relations that focused on the external rather than the internal behaviour of countries, emphasised the need to prevent a rupture in Sino-American ties despite the end of the Soviet threat that had united the two countries during the Cold War. However, while George H.W. Bush's system was less formal than Nixon's, it also was centralised to the White House and a few key advisers the president trusted. Thus one could see a far greater role to the White house as he made an exception to the ban on high level visits and sent his secretary of State James Baker to visit Beijing for consultations on the question of ending sanctions and the loan from the World Bank.

The US-China Relations During the Clinton Presidency
On November 1992, the American people elected Bill Clinton as their President, a man pledged to the ideas of conditioning the MFN status on China's meeting American demands on human rights, non-proliferation and a host of other issues. By naming Winston Lord as his Assistant Secretary of State for East Asia and the Pacific, who was very critical of the Chinese government and had step down as the Ambassador to China on the eve of the Tiananmen massacre, he indicated that he would pursue a hard line with the Chinese (Suettinger, 2000).The administration's aggressive policy on human rights also stemmed from a general concept of world order in which China was expected to play a stakeholder's role. This approach, according

to critics of Clinton, did not recognise the difficulty of negotiating with the Chinese after 'seeking to facilitate a peaceful evolution of China from communism to democracy by encouraging the forces of economic and political liberalisation in that great country' (Warren Christopher, Senate confirmation hearings, 1993).

President Clinton had won the Presidential election with the promise to revive the US economy and pay greater attention to domestic issues. It was this very emphasis of his campaign that led him to eventually realise that engaging in a trade war with China would harm the US economic interests and was forced to adopt an open door policy towards China which his administration called 'comprehensive engagement'. Records show that his administration argued that there was a strong case for negotiated terms for China's entry into the World Trade Organization (WTO), with Permanent Normal Trade Relations. Further, the administration argued that the delinking was the most constructive breakthrough in US-China relations since normalisation in 1979. They believed that by doing so, the US will entangle China more deeply in a rules-based international system and change China internally.

It must also be mentioned that the split between the economic and political departments in the Clinton administration led to a situation where the US found itself bargaining with Beijing in the final weeks before the MFN deadline to make enough modest concessions to justify extension of the same. Eventually, it led Clinton to promise that the US would pursue human rights progress by supporting NGOS in China and encouraging best business practices.

It became clear that the new emphasis in American policy towards China would be driven mainly by economic interests with American business eager to find their fortunes in China. In line with this thinking, on May 26, 1994, despite the poor record of human rights in China, the Clinton Administration decided to delink human rights improvement and trade relations.

President Clinton's decision to extend China's MFN trade status on June 01, 1994, was a turning point in the development of the US-China relations, including trade ties between the two countries. The decision was an important step towards depoliticising US-China economic relations, and it created a new era of further trade expansion between the two nations (Huan, 1997).Clinton by his comprehensive engagement was in favor of market access with an emphasis on global economic integration. As he remarked to the US institute of Peace in April, 1999, on the eve of Premier Zhu Rhongji's visit to the US, "... the purpose of engagement, not to insulate our relationship from the consequences of Chinese action, but to use our relationship to influence China's action in way that advances our values and our interests."

The Clinton Presidency, which adopted the policy of 'comprehensive engagement' towards China, often used presidential authority to grant waivers on numerous items. On August 24, 1993, a report submitted by the then US Under-secretary of State for International Security Affairs, stated that China's Ministry of Aerospace Industry and Pakistan's Ministry of Defence had engaged in missile technology proliferation activities prohibited under the 1990's Missile Technology Control Regime (MTCR). This resulted in the imposition of sanctions by the US Department of State against the Chinese entities and their subsidiaries. The sanctions were lifted in August 1994 following the visit of the Secretary of State, Warren Christopher, to Beijing in which an agreement was reached on the issue with China reaffirming its commitment to the MTCR guidelines. Until 1993 China was denied access to high performance computers, however, by 1995 President Clinton began to loosen export controls.

President Bill Clinton visited China on June 1998, becoming the first President to do so since the Tiananmen Square incident. He criticised the violent crushing of the 1989 demonstrations and urged China to respect and preserve the basic human rights of its people. During this visit, in order to reassure the Chinese of the American commitment to one China Policy, Clinton strongly reaffirmed his 'three No's' policy:

• No support for Taiwan independence
• No recognition of a separate Taiwanese Government
• No backing for Taiwanese membership of international organisations

- While the trip was considered a success, it nevertheless failed to foster agreement on economic reforms that China needed to meet to gain entry into the WTO

During the entire Clinton Presidency, the US continued to engage China on several fronts. Yet, critics pointedly berated Clinton for proliferation of weapons of mass destruction in Asia through China's illegal transfers along with the deepening trends of globalisation which rendered China both economically and militarily modernised. Assessment of Clinton's China policy reveals that a growing number of accusers argued that President Clinton betrayed his country when he allowed massive transfers of American secrets to the Chinese in exchange for illegal contributions to his re-election campaign. According to this view, "It was through Bill Clinton's efforts that the Chinese launched American communications satellites and it was his efforts that made it possible for the Chinese to improve their guidance systems of its rockets and long-range nuclear missiles. Many of them pointed out that until recently, China's space programme was largely a failure ... that was until May 02, 1998 when they successfully launched a Chinese Long March 2C rocket carrying two US satellites into space. Their success was made possible by technical assistance from the US. It should be noted that Bernard Schwartz, the chairman of Loral Space and Communications, one of the firms that sold satellites to the Chinese, was the Democratic Party's largest contributor in 1996." The Report of the Select Committee on US National Security and Military/Commercial Concerns with the People's Republic of China, commonly known as the Cox Report after Representative Christopher Cox, issued a classified US government document reporting on the People's Republic of China's covert operations within the US during the 1980s and 1990s.

Debates in the US revealed deep skepticism of Clinton's policy of comprehensive engagement with China. As illustrated by the influential, *Foreign Policy* magazine, in its November-December 2000 issue on '*Clinton's Foreign Policy*', opinion of Clinton's record as world leader was sharply divided. While many supporters saw pragmatic leadership and bold innovation, critics saw improvised solutions that left America adrift. Both sides saw his handling of China as vitally important. In fact, experts argued that just as the Soviet-US relations characterised the past, the US-China relations would define the next century as the Asia Pacific region will dictate events in a post Cold War world (Hass, 1997). In terms of domestic dynamics, the major focus of Clinton administration China policy culminating in the signing of the US-China Relations Act of 2000 faced a long campaign of opposition from labour, human rights, and conservative groups who wanted to retain the annual review of trade relations with China. The bill survived a bruising battle in the House of Representatives in May, and was passed by the Senate on September 19, 2000.

Washington Post reported that Clinton's decision came after an intensive, sometimes fractious, debate within the administration over what steps to take and how. "At one point, the president was leaning toward extending the trade privileges, but putting sanctions on a range of military-made products. The Treasury and Defence departments vehemently objected, and from the outset the president's economic advisers argued that trade and human rights should not be linked."

Ultimately, Clinton policy was in tune with those who argued that the growth of international institutions in Asia and the expansion of both US and Chinese participation in them would draw the US and China into a thickening web of ties that would promote contact, communication and, over time, greater mutual understanding and even trust, or at the very least, a reduced likelihood of gross misperception. It was no coincidence that China's membership in formal, international governmental organisations more than doubled between 1977 and 1997 (from 21 to 52), while its membership in international non-governmental organisations during the same period grew from 71 to 1,163.

The Clinton years, thus, resolved the battles between the political and economic departments on the emphasis in the China policy. It started with the assumption of the success of a unilateral carrots and sticks policy (starting with conditional ties and MFN) but recognised the dangers of deadlock and confrontation.

The US-China Relations During the George W. Bush Presidency

Presidential candidate George W. Bush positioned himself in the 2000 campaign as a President who would lead the country with 'compassionate conservatism' at home, and a strong American values abroad. According to George W. Bush, America in the 21st century is subjected to new threats that are due to the spread of missile technology and weapons of mass destruction. During his campaign he often mentioned the Chinese missile threat and emphasised the need for more political and religious freedom in China. Bush made it clear that he would not continue Clinton's idea of 'strategic ambiguity', but would be straightforward with China (Stein, 2001).

While Bush strongly believed in open trade with China, he also made it clear that if China would threaten the stability of its region, and especially the fledging Taiwanese democracy, it would find 'a strategic competitor' in the US. On November 19, 1999, Bush delivered his speech on foreign policy outside the Reagan Library in California. When it came to China, he said, "China should be seen as a competitor, not a partner and treated without ill will but without illusions." In August 2000, the election outline that was adopted by the Republican National Convention once again defined China as a 'strategic competitor of the US' and 'key challenge of the US in Asia'. Evidence of this approach appeared in the testimony of John Bolton, the then Undersecretary of State for Arms Control and International Security, to the House of International Relations Committee on June 04, 2003. He stated that the Bush administration imposed sanctions related to unconventional weapons and missiles proliferation 278 times against 197 foreign entities. The number of sanctions invoked annually by the Bush Jr. administration had oscillated but averaged about 35 times per year. In comparison, the Clinton administration averaged eight sanctions annually (Boese, 2008).

During the first term of the Bush administration, a large number of Chinese entities were penalised, as 62 of the 108 sanctions imposed by the State Department involved Chinese entities (Boese, 2008). However, the deepening tensions over North Korea and China's own concerns about militant Islam in Asia after September 11, 2001 brought the two powers closer and as such, China transcended from being America's 'strategic competitor' and a threat to all of Asia, to an "'ngaging partner' whose involvement in world affairs was sorely needed (Moens, 2004). During the President's News Conference with President Jiang Zemin of China in Crawford, Texas, on October 25, 2002; President Bush stated, "The US and China are also allies in the fight against global terror, and our two countries are deepening our economic relations. It is inevitable that nations the size of US and China will have differences, but the President and I agree that we need to resolve our differences through mutual understanding and respect" (Public Papers of the President of the US, 2003).

The George W. Bush administration began by promising a major review of the US' China policy; the major focus would be on how best to compete with China both strategically and economically. Secretary of State Colin Powell while frequently emphasising that the 'US-China relations are at their best since 1972', still argued that the 'China-US relationship is too complex to be described by a single term or a single statement'. It seemed as though the Sino-US relationship was perceived to be strong enough to sustain significant differences and divergences. The Bush Administration also promised that the 'one China policy' will not be changed. However, he also stated that the US 'opposes any unilateral decisions by China or Taiwan to change the status quo'. As Yuan Peng, Sutter, and Harding argue, mutual understanding had led the Americans from the prevailing mindset of the 'China threat' or 'China's collapse' to a gradual replacement of a more realistic acceptance of 'China's peaceful rise'. As they note further, for Beijing, a more cooperative attitude was beginning to overtake negative feelings about 'American hegemony' (Peng, 2004, Sutter, 2005, Harding, 2005).

Assessing the first term of Bush Presidency, that is, 2001-04, it is evident that several firsts had taken place. For instance, rarely had the US simultaneously enjoyed good relations with both Japan and China, as it did then. The same might be said, as Sutter argued, for US relations with China and Taiwan, and with India and Pakistan. Harding, highlighting the 'intriguing mixture of change and continuity' in the Bush approach toward Asia, noted that the administration had completely abandoned the phrase 'strategic competitor', the rubric that Candidate Bush routinely employed in describing China.

While the positive trends in the US-China relations were expected to continue over the course of a second Bush administration, problem areas were also identified as having the potential to do immense harm. For instance, tensions over energy security, Taiwan, and the perpetuation of nationalism within China continued to sour the relationship. In contrast, to the political and economic maturity of their relationship, the military and trade relations between the two were seen to be posing a threat to stable relations.

However, as the crisis on Taiwan Straits erupted with Taiwanese President Chen Shui-bian and his supporters trying to change Taiwan's status vis-a-vis China in ways that risked US confrontation and military conflict with China, the US policymakers 'settled on a policy that endeavored to deter China from using force against Taiwan and deter Taiwan from taking provocative steps toward independence. The main alternatives to this approach seemed less acceptable to US policy makers under prevailing conditions, suggesting that US policy is likely to persist with a dual deterrence policy for the rest of President Bush's term in office' (Sutter, 2006).

Bush began his second term with signs of mounting friction between Washington and Beijing. Alarm over the possible lifting of the European arms embargo helped to draw renewed attention to the pace and scope of China's military build-up. Frustration with stalled negotiations over North Korea's nuclear weapons programme caused some observers to question whether Beijing truly shared the US commitment to halting proliferation. Reports of a PRC diplomatic 'charm offensive' in Southeast Asia stirred fears of waning US influence and incipient Chinese regional hegemony. Evidence showing China as expanding its interactions with Europe, Latin America, Africa, and the Middle East raised the spectre of a new global rivalry for power and influence. To this combustible mix was added an official spat over trade balances and currency values, as well as a flurry of sensational news stories about the impact of China's extraordinary demand on world prices of energy and materials and the planned purchases of US Companies by their new rivals. US policy began then to 'Caution, Cajole, and Cooperate with Beijing'. Beginning in 2006, the US and China agreed to hold regular high-level talks about economic issues and other mutual concerns by establishing the China-US strategic economic dialogue, which meets biannually. Rising economic nationalism in both countries, a point the leaders of the two delegations noted, helped the Bush administration establish the high-level US-China Senior Dialogue to discuss international political issues and work out solutions.

However, the existence of a heavily politicised and divisive US policymaking process towards Beijing made the administration stumble for a while before it built the internal consensus necessary to sustain an overall strategic approach to China. For instance, among the officials responsible for Asia-Pacific affairs, Deputy Secretary of State Richard Armitage, Assistant Secretary of State for Asia-Pacific Region James Kelly, and Senior Director for Asian Affairs, National Security Council, Torkel L. Patterson were all Japan experts, while Deputy Defence Secretary Paul Wolfowitz was an Indonesia expert. There were no serious China experts, which clearly demonstrated the tendency to outweigh Japan against China. On the policy on China, evidence points to three views that existed in the Bush administration—(1) represented by Secretary of State Colin Powell advocated engagement with China, "China, though not a strategic partner, is not an inevitable and unconvertible enemy;" (2) represented by Secretary of Defence Donald Rumsfeld insisted on adopting a hard-line in dialogues with China, holding the view that China's military power, strategic intent, Taiwan policy, as well as the proliferation of weapons of mass destruction pose a great threat on the US, and (3) led Deputy Secretary of State Robert Zoellick's concept of China becoming a 'responsible international stakeholder' provided the intellectual underpinnings of the Bush engagement policy. Secretary of Treasury Paulson as well as President Bush appeared to focus on the economic goals.

Zoellick's concept of engaging China had some important assumptions and policy outcomes. First, the stakeholder concept expected 'China to assume a greater global role and responsibility for addressing a broad array of global governance issues. Second, it therefore implicitly recognised China as a global actor (if not power), and thus, redefined the Sino-American relationship as a global one—not merely as a bilateral or regional Asian relationship. Third, by calling on China to be a global partner of the US, it implicitly rejected the view among the hawks in the administration that China needed to be 'contained' (Shambaugh, 2011). The 'responsible international stakeholder' concept led to deepening institutionalisation of US-China relations, as it stimulated the 'Senior Dialogue' between Zoellick (later Deputy Secretary Negroponte) and Executive Vice Foreign Minister (now State Councillor) Dai Bingguo. The Senior Dialogue, in turn, spawned a series of regional and functional dialogues on different parts of the world and pressing functional issues.

Despite Zoellick's formulation, there nonetheless remained a strong contingent (mainly in the Pentagon) who argued that China needed to be 'hedged' against, given its military modernisation programme and uncertainty about its strategic intentions (and lack of transparency of both). Led by Rumsfeld, the US strategic goals concentrated on strengthening alliances in Asia, establishing non-allied military partnerships with nations all around China, and unilaterally building up US forces in the Pacific, Indian Ocean, and west coast of the continental US. Thus, despite the 'engagement' element of Zoellick's vision, there remained an element of strategic hedging in Bush's China policy. Given this dualistic nature of engaging and hedging, US-China relations remained vulnerable to instability. At a more fundamental level, the Bush period witnessed two important beginnings—(1) divergence in Chinese and American assessments on how to deal with terrorism, and (2) the re-establishment of a central role for China in regional and world affairs. It also consolidated the Chinese quest for equal partnership based on its financial and economic capacities.

Ultimately, towards the end of Bush's administration, Henry M. Paulson Jr., who was the US Treasury Secretary argued, "President Bush engaged Beijing and did so based on the recognition of China's twin priorities—territorial integrity and economic growth. Even if it were possible to block China's growth, it would not be in the US' interest to try. China's rapid emergence as a global economic power presents numerous challenges on issues ranging from trade and investment to commodity markets and the environment. But the inextricable interdependence of China's growth and that of the global economy requires a policy of engagement. In fact, the overriding importance of economic growth to China's leaders presents the best means of influencing China's emergence as a global power and encouraging its integration into the international system."

The US-China Relations and the Obama Presidency

In 2008, Senator Barack Obama, the then Democratic nominee for the US President wrote on what would be his administration's policy towards China. He acknowledged the fact that since the 1970s, America's policy of engaging China had produced major benefits for both sides and for Asia overall. He understood that the US-China relationship has had its share of challenges, and new ones will inevitably emerge especially in a world of common security, where events in any corner of the globe can affect the entire planet. He stated that his administration will seek to revitalise America, and lead it to realise its full potential for constructive engagement in Asia and in the global arena (Obama, 2008).

Obama's policy positions reflected the current complexity of US-Chinese ties. On the one hand, candidate Obama argued that only when political liberalization would take hold in China would China reach its full potential as a nation. Obama also noted the need for the US both to monitor China's growing military capabilities and to press its leadership to end its support for authoritarian regimes such as those in Myanmar (Burma), Sudan, Iran, and Zimbabwe. Obama's campaign statements strongly condemned the Chinese government's March 2008 crackdown on Tibetan protestors and suggested his administration would be tougher in negotiations with Beijing than the Bush administration had been, especially in the area of currency exchange rates. Importantly, not unlike presidential candidates before him, Obama declared that China is neither a friend nor an enemy but a 'competitor'. At the same time, however, Obama also said the US should welcome China's continuing emergence as a world power and work to have a constructive relationship with the country.

Obama stated that although there would be differences, these differences 'should not prevent progress in areas where our interests intersect', such as in an area like climate change. Senator Obama indicated that his administration would continue to provide Taiwan with necessary military equipment, would seek to strengthen 'channels of communication' between Taipei and

Washington, and he called on China to ease Taiwan's international isolation. Like Bush, Obama's policy towards China and Taiwan would be based on the Three US-China communiqués and the Taiwan Relations Act. During his campaign Obama supported US-Taiwan military relations, and declared, "I will do all that I can to support Taiwan's democracy in the years ahead" (Obama, 2008).

Following Barack Obama's election as the President of the US, Asian states looked to him to restore relationships that had been tarnished by George W. Bush's selective engagement and belligerent war on terror, yet expected him to continue Bush's favourable legacies of an enhanced relationship with China, Japan and India, as well as the Six-Party Talks (SPT) in dealing with North Korea's nuclear programme. Obama appointed two Chinese Americans in his cabinet: Steven Chu, Secretary of Energy, and Gary Locke, Secretary of Commerce. In the first 100 days of his administration, Obama sent Secretary of State Hillary Clinton to Japan, Indonesia, South Korea, and China. Many argue that Clinton's trip marks the US recognition of the significance of the so called 'Asian Century'.

Obama, like his two predecessors in the Oval Office, dropped his tough rhetoric he had in the campaign toward the PRC. His statements about China being a competitor or the need to force currency revaluations changed to backing a full engagement and came more quickly than with either Presidents Bush or Clinton. Speculation on whether it was given slightly higher priority, gained credence with Secretary Clinton taking the lead in the effort. She emphasised a 'positive, cooperative, and comprehensive US-China relationship for the 21st Century' (Clinton, 2009). This declaratory policy had practical policy substance. For example, the US-China Strategic and Economic Dialogue in late July 2009 where President Obama declared that 'the relationship between the US and China will shape the 21st century, which makes it as important as any bilateral relationship in the world'. Further, the Obama Administration made efforts to foster common interests in areas as diverse as nuclear non-proliferation, climate change, energy security, trade friction and currency, human rights and religious freedom, and transparency in military affairs (Schmitt, 2009). Both states have agreed to manage their maritime disputes through the Military Maritime Consultative Agreement.

Overall, it appears that Obama has continued the Bush administration's 'two-pronged strategy' by maintaining the US presence in the region to hedge Chinese military power, and at the same time, seeking more cooperation and a proactive role by China in helping to solve the world problems as a responsible stakeholder.

The retaining of the hedging strategy outlined by the Bush administration in the 2006 National Security Strategy was indicated by Secretary of Defence Robert Gates that the US will 'project its power and help its allies in the Pacific by increasing its ability to strike from over the horizon and employ missile defences' to face China's extensive military development. The Obama administration has also adopted a more stringent stance in dealing with trade disputes with China by deciding to impose punitive tariffs on all car and light truck tyres from China. China strongly opposed the decision and responded by raising the issue of 'grave trade protectionism', and accusing the US of breaking commitments made during the G-20 Summit. Furthermore, the US bill imposing new tariffs on the import of solar panels to the US, including from China, contributes to further tension. Additionally, after initially refusing to meet the Tibetan spiritual leader in October 2009, Obama later held a closed meeting with the Dalai Lama in Washington, followed by a meeting between Dalai Lama and Secretary Clinton. The meetings prompted serious Chinese concern, with China's official statement describing the meetings as an intrusion into China's domestic affairs that seriously damaged US-China relations. These developments pose a challenge to the US-China growing positive bilateral relationship (Rahawestri, 2010).

The element of engaging China was visible in the November 2009 visit to China by Obama. The Joint Statement that was issued in conclusion was, in the assessment of a leading political scientist studying China, former editor of the China Quarterly and consultant to the US government, offered hope of a renewed positive phase opening in Sino-American relations. In the run-up to the summit, debates in the US media and elsewhere examined the prospects of a US-China 'G-2' emerging between the world's two most powerful nations. The Joint Statement offered evidence of this, as it provided a visionary roadmap for building the relationship on bilateral, regional, and global levels, and more particularly, provided evidence of the international partnership that the Obama administration sought for from Beijing. The Joint Statement also listed a series of new bilateral agreements in science and technology, clean energy, civil aviation, agriculture, public health, space science, and cultural and educational exchanges.

Issues of concern festered and buffeted the US-China relationship throughout 2010. China's assertive foreign policy in the Asian region marked deterioration in Beijing's ties throughout the Asian region—with Australia, Japan, South Korea, ASEAN, and India. China also faced continued difficulties with the European Union over a range of issues. Even China's ties with certain African and Latin American states began to show some strains. Amid this global downturn in Beijing's foreign policy, the US-China relationship foundered on a rapid succession of troublesome issues some of which were:

- Divergent and contentious positions at the UN Climate Change Conference in Copenhagen in December 2009
- President Obama's meeting with the Dalai Lama
- President Obama's decision to authorise US$ 6.4 billion in defensive arms and equipment transfers to Taiwan—resulting in China's suspension of bilateral military-military exchanges (an irritant in its own right) and threats to retaliate against American companies
- The Google controversy and subsequent concerns about internet controls in, and cyber hacking by China
- Tensions over the slow appreciation of the *renminbi*, and continuing concerns that China was manipulating its currency
- China's watering down the UN sanctions against both North Korea and Iran (although Beijing and Washington agreed to compromised language and actions)
- Beijing's cancellation of official talks on non-proliferation and arms control
- A continually ballooning trade deficit with China
- Continuing Chinese violations of intellectual property

- Complaints by American (and other foreign) companies about an increasingly restrictive operating environment in China
- American concerns about subsides behind China's 'indigenous innovation' and state procurement policies
- Deepening concerns over the deterioration of human rights conditions in China—particularly toward Tibetan and Uighur minorities, the harassment of political dissidents, and the continued imprisonment of Hu Jia (awarded the 2008 Andrei Sakharov Prize) and Liu Xiaobo (awarded the 2010 Nobel Peace Prize)
- Chinese concerns over US intelligence collection and surveillance in China's 200 mile Exclusive Economic Zone (EEZ)
- The US naval and air military exercises with South Korean forces in the Yellow Sea
- China's refusal to recognise the findings of a multinational investigation into the sinking of the South Korean warship *Cheonan* or to publicly condemn North Korea for the sinking
- China's refusal to publicly condemn Pyongyang's late-November artillery shelling of the South Korean island Yeongpyong
- China's persistent protection of North Korea and refusal to restrain its provocative neighbour
- China's minimal contributions to the international effort in Afghanistan
- A disappointing Strategic and Economic Dialogue (S&ED) in Beijing in May
- China's newly assertive claims to disputed waters in the East China Sea (vis-a-vis Japan) and South China Sea (vis-a-vis five Southeast Asian claimants), and Beijing's acerbic rejection of Secretary of State Hillary Clinton's offer at the July ASEAN Regional Forum to facilitate initiatives designed to operationalise the 2002 China-ASEAN declaration on the conduct of parties in the South China Sea (Shambaugh, 2011).

When Chinese President Hu Jintao met with the US President Barack Obama in January 2011, agreements to hold drills on humanitarian assistance and disaster relief, as well as counter-piracy, and to work toward holding more traditional military exercises in the future boded well as they have eased some fears in the region that relations between the US and China were on the verge of a downward spiral. President Obama reassured his Chinese counterpart that the US is not seeking to 'contain' China, and the Chinese president said that Beijing recognized the US role in the Asia-Pacific region. Also notable in the January 19, 2011, 'China–US Joint Statement' were the limited impetus given to military-to-military exchanges; reaffirmation that the goal of both leaders was 'strengthening bilateral relations, addressing regional and global challenges, building a comprehensive and mutually beneficial economic partnership, and cooperating on climate change, energy and the environment'; both sides underscored in the joint statement their support for increased Cross-Strait 'dialogues and interactions in economic, political, and other fields, and for developing more positive and stable Cross-Strait relations'; the joint statement also called for Sino–American exchanges regarding space and other strategically important domains, including cyber security. There was also an agreement that denuclearization of the Korean Peninsula is important, and China expressed 'concern' regarding the Democratic People's Republic of Korea (DPRK)'s claimed uranium enrichment programme and 'opposition' to all actions inconsistent with the 2005 joint statement [pertaining to the Korean Peninsula]; also important have been China's support or no obstruction of various UN resolutions regarding Iran and most recently Libya (Lampton, 2011).

The US Chairman of the Joint Chiefs of Staff Adm. Mike Mullen visited China on July 2011. He met with the Chief of General Staff of the PLA Chen Bingde and future Chinese President Xi Jinping. Mullen's visit has attracted attention because the two sides have recognized that this was an area that had high priority. Resumption of sustained military communication and exchanges, without disruptions arising from intractable differences such as American military support for Taiwan remains an elusive aspect that characterises the relationship. The renewed engagement is also notable because it follows recent incidents and conflicts, which show regional animosities—in the Koreas, the East and South China Seas, and Southeast Asia—threatening to spill out of their former containers, especially where American power is not considered to be overwhelming. It is this aspect that acted as driver to the American approach to a rising China. With containment ruled out, the Asia pivot policy that was announced by Secretary Clinton contained elements of renewed American engagement in the region through regional initiatives that would impact China.

Despite these pressing issues dominating the relationship, the US-China engagement was described by the National Security Adviser Tom Donilon as 'productive and constructive'. Donilon also stressed that Washington was engaged in dealing directly with China on many economic and other themes, "We have a very complicated and quite substantial relationship with China across the board," further adding that "We are ... in an important conversation with them about economics which we think is important for the region and important for the US." He said that the US had been 'quite direct with the Chinese about our strategy' and that Beijing understood Washington was serious about sustaining a more active presence in the region to help ensure its stability and peace (Donilon, 2011).

It was clear that the Obama administration wanted to distinguish its approach from the Bush Administration. Led by Secretary Clinton who was critical of the Strategic Economic Dialogue launched by former Treasury Secretary Henry Paulson during the Bush administration, the Obama administration announced at the Obama-Hu meeting in London that a bilateral 'Strategic and Economic Dialogue' would be commenced, with the first round scheduled to take place in Washington in June 2011. On the US side, the new dialogue mechanism was jointly headed by Secretary of State Clinton and Treasury Secretary Tim Geithner. One can argue quite correctly, that it was the State Department that wanted to be at the forefront of the US-Asia policy and especially China policy.

While the first two years of Obama administration was not plagued by infighting that impacted US' China policy, it nevertheless witnessed significant change on the strategic agenda regarding China. Three important holdover issues: Taiwan, Iran, and North Korea, along with China's compliance with US and international trade rules, saw the merger of both strategic and economic interests at the core of American agenda. Kurt Campbell, Assistant Secretary, Bureau of East Asian and Pacific Affairs US Department of State, in his testimony to the House Committee on Foreign Affairs stated, "US government will continue to press China for demonstrable progress on economic issues, including further advancements on trade and investment and full implementation of commitments it made during President Hu's visit on trade, investment, and economic rebalancing, including exchange rate reform"(Campbell.2012). He added that "...as a Pacific power. The Obama Administration, following a long history of bipartisan commitment to Asia, has articulated a five-part framework for our engagement in the AsiaPacific: First, deepen and modernize our alliances with Japan, the Republic of Korea, Australia Thailand and the Philippines. Second, broaden our engagement with increasingly important partners like Indonesia, Vietnam, Mongolia, New Zealand, Singapore, Malaysia, and most notably India. Third, develop a predictable, stable, and comprehensive relationship with China. Fourth, engage and invest in the region's burgeoning multilateral architecture. And, fifth pursue a confident and aggressive trade and economic strategy." (Ibid.)

Historically, the US has played a crucial role in the security, political, and economic affairs of the Asia Pacific region. the US foreign policy concerns in Asia included issues and challenges of security in the Korean peninsula and the Afghanistan-Pakistan border to US relations with China, India, and Association of South East Asian Nations (ASEAN). However, since 9/11, the US' Asia policy emphasised the priorities in the Middle East and South Asia in the context of the Global War on Terror (GWOT). By the end of the first decade of twenty first century however, US once again shifted its gaze to shaping the fundamentals of its Asia policy. The announcement of the pivot towards Asia served to crystallise the American perception of Asia's importance into realistic policy.

America's shift in its Asia policy in the current context has also the distinction of being supported by a bipartisan consensus in the political sphere whether in the Congress or in the Pentagon. Alluding to this bipartisan consensus that exists among US leaders regarding the key elements of the US foreign policy toward Asia, reports point out that it 'included recognition of the region's growing importance in the world, the need to maintain a US military presence in Asia, and the importance of avoiding a military clash with China through a combination of deterrence and defence measures'.

The US maritime strategy of 2007 had officially began to underline US' seriousness towards the region as a whole and China in particular. Titled 'A

Cooperative Strategy for 21st Century Sea power', this was presented to maritime leaders from more than 100 countries attending the International Sea power Symposium at the Naval War College at Newport, RI. It outlined six imperatives as reported by the Washington Post, "These include the traditional missions of concentrating major combat forces in the Persian Gulf, Indian Ocean and Western Pacific to deter or fight potential conflicts." Protecting vital sea lanes represents a growing priority, it said, as seaborne trade has more than quadrupled over the last four decades and now accounts for 90 per cent of all international commerce and two-thirds of global petroleum trade. In other words:

- limit regional conflict with forward deployed, decisive maritime power.
- deter major power wars.
- win US' wars.
- contribute to homeland defence in depth.
- foster and sustain cooperative relationships with more international parties.
- prevent or contain local disruptions before they impact the global system.

According to Commander Tim Day, a former naval officer and expert at the US Naval War College, "The Maritime Strategy stresses coalition building for a variety of purposes, from counter piracy and counter proliferation to humanitarian and disaster relief. These are worthy missions. But the document's drafters tucked away a couple of bloody-minded passages in the text. The first directs the sea services to remain capable of imposing 'local sea control' in any navigable body of water on the face of the earth. The US will do this by itself if necessary. Evidently it's hard to give up the habit of ruling the waves, wherever those waves may be found.

"But the second proclaims that the Navy, Marines, and Coast Guard have fixed their strategic gaze on maritime Asia. They will stage 'credible combat power' in two oceans—the Western Pacific and the greater Indian Ocean—for the foreseeable future. Their intention to remain Number One in this grand 'Indo-Pacific' theatre. What this means is that the US Navy will remain the two-ocean navy it's been since 1940, when Congress passed the Two-Ocean Navy Act—in effect creating one navy for the Atlantic and a second for the Pacific. But the second ocean is now the Indian Ocean. It's more accurate to say the navy is pivoting from the Atlantic to the Indian Ocean." http://thediplomat.com/author/james-holmes/

As a result of this strategic thinking, President Obama announced a naval base in Darwin Australia in 2011. Indeed it may be argued that the Obama administration's adoption of a policy of rebalancing toward Asia involves detailed strategic, economic, trade, human rights and diplomatic initiatives. It is also indicative that the US plans to play a leadership role in Asia for many years to come. While many aspects of this policy are not new, scrutiny of its likely impact on the US-China relations and its implications for others in the region particularly India, Indonesia, Australia. South Korea and Japan need to be calculated. Firstly, President Barack Obama's decision to rotate 2,500 US Marines through a base in northern Australia was an early sign of that pivot. Secondly, in the November Asia-Pacific Economic Cooperation meeting, held in Obama's home state of Hawaii, the US promoted a new set of trade talks called the Trans-Pacific Partnership. Both events reinforce Obama's message to the Asia-Pacific region that the US intends to remain an engaged power (Nye, 2011).

Any assessment of the rebalancing or pivot policy must start with the understanding that it appears to be an adjustment to a long-standing US approach to the complexities of East Asia. Quoting the formulation of Prof. Thomas Christensen of Princeton University, who was a deputy assistant secretary of state in the George W. Bush administration with responsibility for China, is worthwhile, "Rather than trying to rollback or contain the growth of Chinese power, the US has used the combination of a strong US regional presence and a series of creative diplomatic initiatives to encourage Beijing to seek increased influence through diplomatic and economic interactions rather than coercion, and to use that increased influence in a manner that improves the prospects for security and economic prosperity in Asia and around the world."

Thus, the nature of US response to a rising China is based on how the US will set boundaries for Chinese expansion regionally along with dealing directly on economic and military issues. As pointed out by an expert, "US will best shape China's future course in a positive way through a regional presence that sets boundaries and by exploiting the opportunities provided by shared and overlapping interests. Such an approach does not reject the revival of China as a great power. Far from it. But it seeks to increase the odds that China's revival will be constructive" (Richard C. Bush III, Director, Center for Northeast Asian Policy Studies, Brookings, January 31, 2012). Asia's importance to the US is also highlighted by its impressive economic performance over the last two decades in particular. As Secretary of State Hillary Clinton put it, "The Asia-Pacific has become a key driver of global politics. Stretching from the Indian subcontinent to the western shores of the Americas, the region spans two oceans—the Pacific and the Indian—that are increasingly linked by shipping and strategy. It boasts almost half the world's population. It includes many of the key engines of the global economy, as well as the largest emitters of greenhouse gases. It is home to several of our key allies and important emerging powers like China, India, and Indonesia.

"At a time when the region is building a more mature security and economic architecture to promote stability and prosperity, US commitment there is essential. It will help build that architecture and pay dividends for continued American leadership well into this century..." (Hillary Clinton, 2011) and further stated, "...we are also building new partnerships to help solve shared problems. Our outreach to China, India, Indonesia, Singapore, New Zealand, Malaysia, Mongolia, Vietnam, Brunei, and the Pacific Island countries is all part of a broader effort to ensure a more comprehensive approach to American strategy and engagement in the region. We are asking these emerging partners to join us in shaping and participating in a rules-based regional and global order."

In particular, Pentagon's January 2012 strategic guidance paper calls for 'investing in a long-term strategic partnership with India to support its ability to serve as a regional economic anchor and provider of security in the broader Indian Ocean region'. Both Obama during his visit to India in November 2010 and Secretary of State Hillary Clinton during her trip in 2011 have called on New Delhi to play a more active strategic role in East Asia. In effect, the pivot or rebalancing would affect both China and India quite substantially.

For the US, both China and India are, apart from being two huge markets offering economic benefits and opportunities, also of strategic value. China and India are also two transitional countries demonstrating uncertainty, from the US' strategic point of view. What Washington fears most is the possibility of China's interests clashing with the creation of a new international liberal politico-economic order in a multi-polar world. How the US actually calculates the China factor in this ongoing policy change, will thus remain central to Asia and beyond.

Conclusion

The great power shift of the 21st century has been the return of Asia to the centre of world affairs. In it, the rise of China will likely be the most important international relations story, but it remains unclear whether that story will have a happy ending. Will China's ascent increase the probability of great-power war? Will an era of the US-China tension be as dangerous as the Cold War? Will it be even worse, because China, unlike the Soviet Union, will prove a serious economic competitor as well as a geopolitical one? These questions remain the reason for the discussion so far on US-China relations in the past four decades. In particular, the importance of China for the US went well beyond the Cold War as the bilateral relationship rested on China's unique qualities, past behaviour, and economic trajectory.

Two distinct schools of thought have broadly characterised the US approach to China since normalisation in 1972. One set belongs to those who saw merit in deep constructive engagement as a way of bringing China into the international order, while the other argued that China's rise and economic growth will need to be hedged by creating a balance of power around it. The policy options were thus based on a complex interplay between these two assumptions. Under various administrations, domestic wrangling and infighting in the executive branch, partisan politics of the Congress and the ideological preferences of the Presidency played a distinct role in shaping the agenda and strategy towards China. Thus, from Nixon to George W. Bush, the China debate in the US government has pitted liberal optimists against pessimistic realists.

The liberals argue that because the post Cold War international order is defined by economic and political openness, it can accommodate China's rise peacefully. According to this argument, the US and other leading powers, can and will make clear that China is welcome to join the existing order and prosper within it, Further, China is likely to join the system rather than launch a costly and dangerous struggle to overturn it to establish an order more to its own liking.

In contrast, the standard realist views predict intense competition as China grows. Strength and power, most realists argue, will lead it to pursue its interests more assertively, which will in turn lead the US and other countries to balance against it. This cycle could possibly generate at the least a parallel to the Cold War standoff between the US and the Soviet Union, and perhaps even a hegemonic war. Adherents of this view have pointed to China's recent harder line on its maritime claims in the East China and South China seas, and advocated hedging and balancing, The increasingly close relations between the US and India is interpreted as signs that the assumption of cycle of assertiveness and balancing has already begun.

The US-China relationship is no longer confined to the realm of foreign policy exchanges that are handled at the diplomatic level. Instead, issues ranging from trade, technology transfers on dual use items, product safety, and the environment are amongst the many that now characterise the US-China relationship. It appears evident that successive US administrations from Nixon to the present Obama administration have consistently pursued economic engagement as a stabilising force in the US-China bilateral relations and as a liberalising force within Chinese society. It seems increasingly clear that support for the continuation of this policy may hinge on whether this policy of engagement has helped secure Chinese cooperation in meeting vital regional and international security challenges. Economic leverage did have its utility for Washington in gaining Chinese concession in some economic and non-proliferation disputes. The Sino-American economic relationship provided the essential glue that held the countries together while Washington and Beijing attempted to rebuild a new, broad-based rationale for long-term cooperation.

The recent hedge and balance approach in the pivot policy, however, has the imprint of those American strategists who argue that Chinese policy pursues two long-term objectives—(1) displacing the US as the pre-eminent power in the western Pacific, and (2) consolidating Asia into an exclusionary bloc deferring to Chinese economic and foreign policy interests.

The combination of these two approaches has led to the situation where on the one hand there is a direct S&ED with the Chinese annually, and a defence strategy that draws regional boundaries through alliances and rely on aiding friendly states, deterrence, containment, and far more limited and less costly forms of intervention.

As the US heads for another set of presidential elections in 2012, the China debate has once again raised its head. Yet again the candidates from both sides are accusing the other of either accommodation or acquiescence to China.

The US-China relations are entering a critical juncture. Two days after the November 06 vote, China will begin its own once-in-a-decade leadership transition. How the next US administration gets on with the new leadership in Beijing could determine whether the world's pre-eminent military powers can cooperate in the Asia-Pacific region or head on a path to confrontation.

Bibliography

- Jan C. Berris and Michael Oksenberg,, "The American View of China in the Twenty-first Century", in David L. Boren and Edward J. Perkins (Eds.), *Preparing America's Foreign Policy for the 21st Century*, University of Oklahoma Press, 1999.

- Lester H. Brune and Dean Richard Burns, *Chronological History of US Foreign Relations: 1932-1988,* (Routledge, 2002-09).

- Zbigniew K. Brzezinski, *Power and Principle: Memoirs of the National Security Advisor 1977-1981,* (Farrar, Straus and Giroux, 1985).

- W. Burr, *The Kissinger Transcripts: The Top Secret Talks with Beijing and Moscow,* (New York: The New Press, 1999).

- Kurt Campbell,, Testimony to the US Congress, House, Committee on Foreign Affairs, Subcommittee on Asia and the Pacific, Oversight Hearings, titled "*Asia Overview: Protecting American Interests in China and Asia*", 2012. http://foreignaffairs.house.gov/hearings/view/?1240

- Warren Christopher, Secretary-Designate Statement before the Senate Foreign Relations

Committee at his Confirmation Hearing, Washington, January 13, 1993, *History of the Department of State During the Clinton Presidency (1993-2001)* released by the Office of the Historian, Bureau of Public Affairs. http://2001-2009.state.gov/r/pa/ho/pubs/8543. htm

- Clinton's Foreign Policy *Foreign Policy* , No. 121 (November-December 2000), pp. 18-20, 22, 24, 26, 28-29, published by *Washington Post Newsweek Interactive, LLC* Article. http://www.jstor.org/stable/1149615

- Bill Clinton, http://edition.cnn.com/ALLPOLITICS/stories/1999/04/07/clinton.china/transcript.html

- Bill Clinton, http://clinton5.nara.gov/WH/Accomplishments/eightyears-10.html

- Hillary Clinton, http://www.foreignpolicy.com/articles/2011/10/11/americas_pacific_century?page=full

- W.I. Cohen, *America's Response to China: A history of Sino-American Relations,* (New York: Columbia University Press, 2000).

- John Franklin Copper, *"Playing With Fire: The Looming War with China Over Taiwan",* (Westport, Connecticut, London: Praeger Security International, 2006).

- Jean A. Garrison, *"Making China Policy: From Nixon to G. W. Bush"* (Boulder, CO: Lynn Reinner, 2005). https://www.rienner.com/uploads/47e014d3366bd.pdf

- John W. Garver, *"Face Off: China, the US and Taiwan's Democratization"* (Seattle: University of Washington Press, 1977), chapter 1.

- Evelyn Goh, Evelyn, *Constructing the US Rapprochement with China, 1961-1974: From 'Red Menace' to 'Tacit Ally'* (New York,Cambridge, UK,: Cambridge University Press, 2005).

- Richard N. Haass, *Fatal Distraction: Bill Clinton's Foreign Policy in Foreign Policy,* no. 108 (Autumn, 1997), pp. 112-123 (Washington Post, Newsweek Interactive, LLC) Article Stable URL: http://www.jstor.org/stable/1149093

- HRobert M. Hathaway and Wilson Lee (eds.), *"George W. Bush and East Asia: A First Term Assessment",* Woodrow Wilson International Center for Scholars, Washington, D.C., 2005. http://www.wilsoncenter.org/sites/default/files/bushasia2rpt.pdf

- Richard Holbrooke, http://www.project-syndicate.org/commentary/opening-china--then-and-now

- John H. Holdridge, *"Crossing the Divide: An insider's account of the normalization of US-China relations",* (New York: Rowman and Littlefield Publishers, 1997).

- G. Huan, *"US-China Trade to the Year 2000",* in Barfield, C.E. (editor), *Expanding US-Asian Trade and Investment: New challenges and policy options,* (Washington D.C.: American Enterprise Institute for Public Policy Research Press, 1997).

- IMF Report. http://www.imf.org/external/pubs/ft/reo/2010/apd/eng/areo0410ex.pdf

- Ramy Inocencio. http://business.blogs.cnn.com/2011/04/27/the-american-age-ends-in-2016/

- J.S.H. Jones, *"The Evolution of China's engagement with International Governmental Organizations: Towards a liberal Foreign Policy?" Asian Survey*, vol. 45, no. 5, (September-October 2005): 702-721.

- Henry Kissinger, *"Does America Need a Foreign Policy: Towards a Diplomacy for the 21ˢᵗ Century"*, (New York : Simon and Schuster, 2001).

- ------------------, *"On China"*, (London: Allen Lane, Penguin Books, 2011).

- -------------- *"The Future of US-Chinese Relations: Conflict Is a Choice, Not a Necessity"*, *Foreign Affairs* - March / April 2012.

- David M. Lampton, *"Slipping Tectonic Plates in US-China Relations: Seeking Stabilization amid Tremors"*, American Foreign Policy Interests: The Journal of the National Committee on American Foreign Policy, July 20, 2011, pp. 111-118.

- James Mann, "About Face: A History of America's Curious Relationship with China, from Nixon to Clinton" (New York: Alfred A. Knopf, 1999).

- Laura Macinnis, *"White House says US-China relationship complicated"*. http://www.reuters.com/article/2011/11/19/us-asia-summit-whitehouse-china-idUSTRE7AI07A20111119 (Accessed on November 27, 2011).

- Memorandum for the Chairman, NSC Senior Review group, Subject NSSM 124: Next Steps towards the People's Republic of China (PRC), April 19, 1971, National Security Archive Electronic Briefing Book no 18. URL: http://www.gwu.edu/~nsarchiv/NSAEBB/NSAEBB19/index.html (Accessed on April 12, 2011).

- A. Moens, *"The Foreign Policy of George W. Bush: Values, Strategy and loyalty"*, (Vermont: Ashgate Publishing Company, 2004).

- Peter V. Ness, *"Bush's search for absolute security and the rise of China"*, in Mark Beeson (Edi), *"Bush and Asia: America's evolving relations with East Asia"*, (New York: Routledge, 2006).

- Joseph Nye, "Obama's Pacific Pivot", Op-Ed, *The Korea Herald,* December 08, 2011. http://belfercenter.ksg.harvard.edu/publication/21610/obamas_pacific_pivot.html?breadcrumb=%2Fpublication%2F701%2Ffuture_of_uschina_relations

- Barrack Obama, *"US-China Policy under an Obama Administration"*, 2008. http://www.amchamchina.org/upload/wysiwyg/ObamaENArticle.pdf (Accessed on November 26, 2011).

- M. Oksenberg and E. Economy, *"Shaping US-China Relations: A long term strategy"*, (New York: Council on Foreign Relations, 1997).

- H.M. Paulson, *"A strategic economic engagement: strengthening US - China ties"*, *Foreign Affairs,* September/October 2008. http://www.foreignaffairs.com/articles/63567/henry-m-paulson-jr/a-strategic-economic-engagement (Accessed on April 12, 2011).

- *Public Papers of the President of the US*, George W. Bush, Book 2, July o1 to December 31, 2001, (Office of the Federal Register National Archive and records Administration:

Washington) 2003.

- Yuan Peng, *"China Policy under the next Bush Administration"*, *China Brief Volume:4, Issue:22.* http://www.jamestown.org/programs/chinabrief/single/?tx_ttnews%5Btt_news%5D=3693&tx_ttnews%5BbackPid%5D=194&no_cache=1

- Simei Qing, *"From Allies to Enemies: Visions of Modernity, Identity and US-China Diplomacy, 1945-1960"*, (Massachusetts: Harvard University Press, 2007).

- Mayang A. Rahawestri, Mayang A. (2010), *"Obama's Foreign Policy in Asia More Continuity than Change"*, 2010. http://www.securitychallenges.org.au/ArticlePDFs/vol6no1Rahawestri.pdf (Accessed on November 26, 2011).

- Robert S. Ross, *"Negotiating Cooperation: The US and China 1969-1989"*, (California: Stanford University Press, 1995).

- Reagan Diaries, quoted in http://www.taipeitimes.com/News/editorials/archives/2007/05/30/2003363123/1.

- Gary J. Schmitt, Gary J. (2009), *"The Obama Administration's Approach to Asia: Early Signals"*, 2009. http://www.aei.org/article/foreign-and-defence-policy/regional/asia/the-obama-administrations-approach-to-asia-early-signals/ (Accessed on November 26, 2011).

- D. Shambaugh, *"Containment or engagement of China? Calculating Beijing's Responses"*, *International Security,* vol. 21, no. 2, (Autumn 1996): 180-209.

- --------------------, *"Stabilizing Unstable US-China Relations? Prospects for the Hu Jintao Visit"*, 2011. http://www.brookings.edu/papers/2011/01_us_china_shambaugh.aspx (Accessed on November 27, 2011).

- --------------------, 2011. http://www.brookings.edu/research/articles/2009/04/china-shambaugh

- Dan Steinbock, *"China's Next Stage of Growth: Reassessing US policy Towards China"*, American Foreign Policy Interests: The Journal of the National Committee on American Foreign Policy, December 13, 2010, pp. 347-362.

- Richard J. Stein, *"US Foreign Policy since the Cold War"*, (New York: H.W. Wilson Company, 2001).

- Stratford, *"A Competitive US-China Engagement"*, 2011. http://www.realclearworld.com/articles/2011/07/13/a_competitive_us-china_engagement_99589.html (Accessed on January 28, 2012).

- Robert L. uettinger, *"The US and China: Tough Engagements"*, in Robert N Hass and Meghan L O'Sullivan (Edi), *Honey and Vinegar: incentives, sanctions and foreign policy,* (Washington D.C.: Brookings Institution Press, 2001).

- Robert Sutter, *"The Taiwan Problem in the Second George W. Bush Administration—US officials' views and their implications for US policy"*, 2006.

- in *Journal of Contemporary China*, 15(48), August 2006, 417- 441. http://facultypages.morris.umn.edu/~joos/us/Readings/2_US%20in%20NE%20Asia/Taiwan%20problem.

pdf

- E.F. Vogel (editor), *"Living with China: US-China relations in the 21ˢᵗCentury"*, (New York: W.W. Norton and Company, 1997).

- Boese Wade, Boese. (2008), *"Type, targets of sanctions shifts in Bush administration"*, *Arms Control Today*, 2008. www.armscontrol.org/act/2008_10/sanctions.htm (Accessed on February 24, 2012).

- White House, Office of the Press Secretary, "US-China Joint Statement", November 17, 2009. http://www.whitehouse.gov/the-press-office/us-china-joint-statement

- Wietz, http://thediplomat.com/2012/05/03/pivot-out-rebalance-in/ Kieth Wilkerson and Christian Crusade, "Who sold Red China our ICBM secrets?" June 1998. http://www. clintonmemoriallibrary.com/clint_foreign.html

- Zhang Quingmin, *"The Bureaucratic Politics of US Arms Sales to Taiwan"*, Chinese Journal of International Politics (2006) 1 (2): 231-265 (Accessed on April 15, 2012).

- http://tech.mit.edu/V114/N27/china.27w.html

- http://www.washingtonpost.com/wp-yn/content/article/2007/10/17/ AR2007101700536_pf.html

6

Henry Kissinger, China, and Third Indo-China War

V. Suryanarayan

"Ideology had disappeared from the conflicts. The communist power centres were conducting a balance-of-power contest based not on ideology but on national interest."

— Kisssinger, *On China*

"There had been an amazing cynicism and duplicity on the Chinese side. And they preach against imperialism and act themselves in the old imperialist and expansionist way, altogether their policy seems to be one of unabashed chauvinism."

— Jawaharlal Nehru,
Speech in Lok Sabha, December 10, 1962

The much awaited book, *On China,* written by scholar diplomat Henry Kissinger, not only makes fascinating reading, it is an invaluable reference material for students of international relations. From July 1971, when Kissinger made his first secret visit to China, he has maintained excellent equations with successive generations of Chinese leaders. He views contemporary history of China as a continuation of the past and describes the rationale behind Chinese thinking, diplomacy, strategy and negotiations.

This essay is a re-evaluation of the Third Indo-China War based on the writings of Henry Kissinger. The author has also referred to the Memoirs of Singapore statesman Lee Kuan Yew, *'From Third World to First: The Singapore Story, 1965-2000',* and the recently published autobiography of former President of Singapore S.R. Nathan, who was associated with the Ministry of Foreign Affairs during the Third Indo-China War. The book is entitled '*An Unexpected Journey, Path to Presidency*'. Few preliminary observations are in order before analysing the subject under scrutiny.

Significance of Vietnamese Revolution

The revolution in Vietnam, under the inspiring leadership of Ho Chi Minh, is one of the most brilliant chapters in the history of the 20th century. With massive aid from both the Soviet Union and China, but with only their reluctant assent and occasionally even against their wishes, the heroic people of Vietnam humbled the US and struck a death blow to imperialism and neo-colonialism. During the Third Indo-China War there was a vicious attempt to distort the true nature of the Vietnamese revolution, malign and vilify the Vietnamese leaders as war mongers and legitimise, in retrospect, the American military intervention in Vietnam. We must be on our guard against this distortion of history.

Sino-Vietnamese Relations—Historical Legacy

Bordering on China both by land and by sea, the northern part of Vietnam was subjected to successive invasions from imperial China and consequent sinicisation of its culture. It may be mentioned that while all other parts of Southeast Asia, including southern part of Vietnam, were subjected to Indian cultural influences North Vietnam came under frequent Chinese domination. Vietnamese national culture, as Kissinger points out, 'came to reflect the legacy of two somewhat contradictory forces; on the one hand, the absorption of Chinese culture; on the other opposition to Chinese political and military domination'. And what is more, resistance to Chinese domination instilled in the Vietnamese a great pride in their separate identity. In fact, two great heroes of Vietnamese history are the two Trung sisters, who rallied their people against Chinese domination, threw off the Chinese yoke and when the Chinese army wanted to reconquer the territory committed suicide by drowning in the river. In February 1973, when Kissinger visited Hanoi in connection with the implementation of the Paris Agreements, Le Duc Tho escorted him to Hanoi's national museum primarily to 'show me the section devoted to Vietnamese struggles against China—still formally an ally of Vietnam'.

After last of the Ming rulers was driven out of Vietnam in the 15th century, a Vietnamese poet composed a poem:

There are no more sharks in the sea

There are no more beasts on earth

The sky is serene

Time is now to build up peace for ten thousand years.

Indo-China Developments After the Second World War

Since the end of the Second World War, the States of Indo-China—Vietnam, Laos and Cambodia—have not enjoyed a sense of security and stable balance of power. During the first Indo-China conflict, spanning from 1945 to 1954, there was the inevitable confrontation between the forces of French imperialism and the resurgent nationalist aspirations of the Indo-Chinese peoples. The Second Indo-China War (1959-75), which began with US intervention first in Vietnam and later in Laos and Cambodia was rationalised as an attempt to defend the 'free world' against 'monolithic communism', but gradually turned out to be a savage war between the US and its client states against the radical nationalist forces in Indo-China. No sooner did the conflict end in 1975, the hitherto concealed antagonisms among the three communist states—Vietnam, Kampuchea, and China—burst into the open, and paved the way for the third Indo-China conflict. The inter-related domestic and international factors made Kampuchea not only a theatre of internecine conflict, but also an area of major international concern.

Transformation in International Scenario-Changing US Stance

Since the mid-1960s, the US had been exploiting the Sino-Soviet differences to its advantage. The US tacitly acknowledged the emergence of China as an independent centre of power and provided political backing to it. In 1964, when the US escalated the Vietnam War, the Johnson administration assured China that it will not violate the latter's air space. China, in turn, gave the guarantee that it will not directly intervene in the Vietnam War. The US fully capitalised on this understanding and intensified the bombing of North Vietnam to compel the Vietnamese to come to the negotiating table. It is worth remembering that the mining of the Haiphong harbour, and the savage bombing of North Vietnam were undertaken immediately after the establishment of China connection in 1972.

How does Kissinger explain the US debacle in Indo China? To quote Kissinger, "America's overriding mistake in the Vietnam War was not what divided the American public; whether the US Government was sufficiently devoted to a diplomatic outcome. Rather, it was the inability to face the fact that a so-called diplomatic outcome, so earnestly—even desperately—sought by successive administrations of both American political parties, required pressure equivalent to what amounted to the total defeat of Hanoi, and that Moscow and Beijing had only facilitating, not a directive role."

The debacle in Indo-China compelled the US to readjust its foreign policy to suit the needs of post-Vietnam War Southeast Asia. The bases in Thailand were dismantled because they had outlived their utility and in the new situation had also become redundant. There was no indication that the US wanted to close down the bases in the Philippines because these bases were vital in ensuring the US supremacy in the Indian and Pacific Oceans. The withdrawal of ground troops from Indo-China was accompanied by the augmenting of naval and air power in the Indian Ocean. Though the US originally intervened in Vietnam to contain Chinese expansionism, the US hostility towards Vietnam continued even after the end of the Vietnam War and the normalisation of the US-China relations. Kissinger puts it in his characteristic frankness, "The US opposed North Vietnam as the spearhead of a Soviet-Chinese design. China supported Hanoi to blunt a perceived American thrust to dominate Asia. Both were mistaken. Hanoi fought only for its own national account." Paul M. Kattenburg has described the continuing animus of the US towards Vietnam, "The US policy towards Vietnam is still driven by a profound animus on the part of the American policy makers towards a country they believe has embarrassed and humiliated the US."

The growing identity of interests between Beijing and Washington was facilitated by both sides to serve their own purposes. It is interesting to note that the Chinese invasion of Vietnam took place only after Deng Xiaoping's visit to the US, and detailed discussions with American policy makers. According to Kissinger, "Deng assumed an identity of strategic interests and concentrated on achieving a parallel implementation."

Deng put it bluntly to Brzezinski, our objective is to cope with the 'polar bear and that is that'. In an interview with the *Time* magazine, Deng advocated a united front against the Soviet Union, "If we really want to be able to place curbs on the polar bear, the only realist thing for us is to unite. If we only depend on the strength of the US, it is not enough. If we only depend on the strength of Europe, it is not enough. We are an insignificant, poor country, but if we unite, well, it will then carry weight." What Deng wanted was not a formal alliance with the US, but promoting of 'parallel interests ... an informal global arrangement to contain the Soviet Union'. Deng's analysis of the strategic situation in Southeast Asia was Vietnam will not stop with the establishment of an 'Indo-Chinese federation'. Kissinger quotes Vice Premier Geng Biao telling Brezezinski, "The Soviet Union's support for Vietnam is a component of its global strategy. It is directed not just against Thailand, but at Malaysia, Singapore, Indonesia and the Straits of Malacca. If they succeeded it should be a fatal blow to ASEAN and also would interdict the lines of communication for Japan and the US. We are committed to do something about this. We may have no capability to cope with the Soviet Union, but we have the capability to cope with Vietnam". "China had an obligation to act," Deng said. "China needed Washington's moral support by which he meant sufficient ambiguity about the American designs to give the Soviets pause." Deng told President Carter, "China must still teach Vietnam a lesson. The Soviet Union can use Cuba and Vietnam, and then Afghanistan will evolve into a proxy (for the Soviet Union). The PRC is approaching this issue from a position of strength. The action will be very limited. If Vietnam thought PRC soft, the situation will get worse."

The US gave tacit support to China in its punitive action against Vietnam in February 1979. The State Department called for the 'immediate withdrawal of Vietnamese troops from Cambodia and Chinese troops from Vietnam', a formulation which implied that the US would not object to Chinese staying in Vietnam as long as the Vietnamese were in Cambodia. The US also warned Moscow not to attack China, seeming to give further cover to Chinese adventure. It was apparent that Beijing during this period wanted the continuing US military presence in Southeast Asia, as it would checkmate its principal adversary the Soviet Union. The US decision was facilitated because the member states of ASEAN wanted the US to retain a credible military presence. They regarded American power, represented by the Seventh Fleet and the air force squadrons in the Philippines, to be the ultimate guarantor of their safety. Thailand and Singapore openly advocated continuing US military presence, while Indonesia and Malaysia were not so vocal. As a result, the US assured ASEAN that it will continue to maintain a credible military presence. In addition the US was also offering substantial military assistance to South East Asian countries to strengthen their defence preparedness.

Soviet Failure to Win Friends in Southeast Asia
From the Soviet Union's point of view, the significance of Southeast Asia arose from its adversarial relations with China, and the necessity to contain the influence of the US. In the 1950s and 1960s, the Soviet Union showed only minimal interest in Southeast Asia, with significant exceptions. The communist-led revolutionary movements, which attempted to seize power in the immediate post-war years, received vocal support from the USSR. In the late 1950s and early 1960s (before the forging of Peking-Jakarta axis and the overthrow of Sukarno in 1965) the Soviet Union provided considerable economic and military aid to Indonesia. Third, and most, important, it had been continuously supporting Vietnam in its struggle against US imperialism, an assistance, it must be pointed out which was conditioned to checkmate the Chinese influence in Indo-China.

Since 1975, the Soviet goal in Southeast Asia had been the containment of Chinese influence and creating, wherever possible, a viable Soviet presence. In the bitter Sino-Soviet dispute for winning friends and influencing people, the Soviet Union had certain positive advantages. Moscow's ability to provide economic aid to the developing regions was considerable. China could never match the Soviet Union in this respect. Secondly, Soviet Union was not 'bowed down' by the burden of the 'Overseas Chinese', who are an object of envy and hatred in many Southeast Asian countries. Thirdly,

Moscow could claim 'greater respectability' as most of the communist parties were aligned to Beijing.

Despite these advantages, Moscow could not make much headway in Southeast Asian capitals. The Soviet drive to sell the 'Collective Security System' did not attract many buyers. The Vietnamese intervention in Kampuchea and Soviet invasion of Afghanistan acted as serious impediments to improved relations. Thailand, the Philippines and Singapore dutifully echoed the US-China view that Vietnam is the 'proxy of Soviet Union' and considered Soviet Union working through Vietnam as the imminent threat to the peace and stability of Southeast Asia.

The major focus of Soviet Union's Southeast Asia policy, therefore, centred around Vietnam. The Soviet objective of limiting China's influence found a natural ally in Vietnam because of Vietnam's burgeoning conflict with China. Soviet policy paid rich dividends. Vietnam joined the Council for Mutual Economic Assistance (COMECON) and entered into a Treaty of Friendship and Co-operation with the Soviet Union. The prolonged war in Kampuchea and the requirements of economic development made Hanoi rely more and more on the Soviet Union. The Soviet Union was the major country which prevented the isolation of Vietnam in the most difficult times of Vietnamese history and the Vietnamese were grateful for it. This did not mean that Soviet Union had a decisive voice in Hanoi's decision making. The Soviet role was one of enabling the Vietnamese to pursue their national objectives, which generally coincided with Soviet objectives in Southeast Asia.

The major question is how did Hanoi view Moscow? After 1975, Hanoi was committed to multiple options and wanted to reduce its dependence on Moscow as the sole arms provider. From the Indian point view, an interesting incident, cited in Nayan Chanda's book, '*Brother Enemy*', needs mention. In the course of an unpublicised visit to New Delhi in June 1975, General Giap made a request to India that it should start an ordnance factory in Vietnam to produce small arms. Unfortunately, Indian response was lukewarm. New Delhi expressed its inability to assist on the ground of lack of resources. Vietnam's relations with the Soviet Union is a subject on whom there are wide differences between Indian observers of Southeast Asian scene and the simplistic view of Kissinger, echoed by many ASEAN countries. My reading of the situation is that the political developments in Indo-China and the hostile polices adopted by US, China, Japan, and ASEAN pushed Hanoi nearer to Moscow. Even then, Hanoi tried to limit Soviet involvement to the minimum. Vietnam had three objectives when China launched its military offensive in February 1979. First, prevent China from gaining a military victory. Second, maintain and consolidate its position in Kampuchea and not be cowed down by Chinese invasion and most important, from the point of view of Vietnam-USSR relations keep the Soviet involvement to the minimum. It is very difficult to accept the proposition that Vietnam is a 'proxy' or 'satellite' of the Soviet Union. A country so intensely nationalist as Vietnam will never be subservient to any country.

China's Policy Towards Indo-China

Reading Kissinger's book one comes to know how obsessed Beijing was with Soviet-Vietnamese co-operation and how dangerous a threat it posed to China's security. It should be recalled that Beijing had always this 'siegementality' that its opponents were encircling it and, therefore, China was bent upon forging new alliances to come out of the isolation and also contain the perceived threat. This time, China's military target was 'a fellow communist country, recent ally, and long time beneficiary of Chinese economic and military support' that did not figure in its consideration. As Kissinger puts it, "The goal was to preserve the strategic equilibrium in Asia, as China saw it. Further China undertook the campaign with the moral support, diplomatic backing and intelligence co-operation of the US—the same 'imperialist power' that Beijing had helped to eject from Indo-China five years earlier."

After 1975, since China's foreign policy came to be dominated by anti-Sovietism, the most serious source of concern was the position of Vietnam. The end of the Vietnam War brought to the surface the long standing differences between the two communist neighbours. A matter of concern for China was the possibility of Vietnam emerging as an independent centre of power, with Soviet support. The fear, in fact, was unfounded for the facts clearly prove that Vietnam was keen to preserve and demonstrate its independence from both China and the Soviet Union and, at the same time, welcome aid from all quarters for the economic rehabilitation of the country. Hanoi was committed to multiple options in order to maximise its independence. During this period, Vietnam turned down the proposal to join the COMECON, because it would have resulted in a breach with China. But since Beijing followed a foreign policy on the assumption that Hanoi and Moscow were potential allies against China, it chose to underwrite and support the Pol Pot regime in Kampuchea against what both China and Kampuchea called 'Vietnamese expansionism'. Vietnam, for its own domestic reasons of rapid economic integration, passed legislation and took administrative steps against the Hoa people and, as a result, the relations between the two countries deteriorated rapidly. The US played a blatantly dangerous role in escalating the Sino-Vietnamese rift. Beijing came out openly against Hanoi only after Brzezinski visited China in May 1978 and denounced 'regional hegemonism' implying the foreign policy of Vietnam. Brzezinski's reference to 'regional hegemony' indicated American support to Chinese action against Vietnam. The US successfully played off Hanoi and Beijing against each other as Vietnam strove for diplomatic recognition and economic aid and China for American technology and support against Soviet Union. The shared concerns about China and the US brought Hanoi and Moscow closer. Events moved swiftly—exodus of the boat people, withdrawal of Chinese technical assistance, Vietnamese entry into the COMECON, Treaty of Friendship and Co-operation with Moscow, Vietnamese entry into Kampuchea and installation of the Heng Samrin Government and China's punitive expedition against Vietnam.

Of all the Chinese leaders, the most bitter against Vietnam was Deng Xiaoping. In a meeting with the Thai leader Kriangsak in November 1977, Deng said, "There is a possibility that Phnom Penh will fall. This would not be the end of the war, but the beginning." Deng strongly hinted that China would resort to punitive steps against Vietnam. The leaders of Singapore concurred with this view. According to S. Rajaratnam, "The Chinese never get emotional, but when Prime Minister Lee Kuan Yew asked Deng about the Vietnamese, I saw in his eyes a glint. I mean real, not simulated. These ungrateful people must be punished. We gave them US$ 20 billion of aid, Chinese sweat and blood and look what happened."

As Kissinger has pointed out, China attacked Vietnam on Feburary 17, 1979 to put 'a restraint on the wild ambitions of the Vietnamese and to give them an appropriate limited lesson'. 'Appropriate' meant to inflict sufficient damage to affect Vietnamese options and calculations for the future; 'limited' meant 'that it would be ended before outside intervention or other factors drove it out of control'. It was also a direct challenge to the Soviet Union. The Indian observers should remember that when China attacked Vietnam it claimed a parallel with Chinese attack on India in 1962 to 'teach a lesson to the other countries'. AB Vajpayee, the Minister of Foreign Affairs, was on an official tour of China at that time and had to cut short his visit. Just as in the case of India, the attack was followed by a retreat.

ASEAN was caught in a dilemma when China attacked Vietnam in early 1979. Having severely criticised Vietnam for occupying Kampuchea, how can ASEAN remain silent on this flagrant violation of Vietnamese sovereignty? As Ambassador Nathan has written, the purpose of Chinese invasion was to 'teach Vietnam a lesson' for invading Cambodia. "Having strongly opposed the Vietnamese invasion of Cambodia, the ASEAN countries had a problem now in coming to terms with Chinese invasion of Vietnam. They could not reasonably endorse it. Fortunately, Chinese troops began to withdraw on March 16, 1979, only a month after the initial attack, and so ASEAN was let off the hook."

Beijing believed that, in the long run, Hanoi will meet its 'Vietnam' in Kampuchea. It wanted to fight Vietnam to the last Kampuchean soldier, and if possible, to the last Thai soldier. With the connivance of the Thai Government, Beijing gave military and economic support to the Khemer insurgents. Beijing also embarked on a programme of recruiting and training Laotian insurgents for acts of subversion in Laos. And more than all these, Beijing kept the Sino-Vietnamese border tense and held out the possibility of a 'second lesson' being taught to Hanoi. In Beijing's calculation, if this 'leechcraft' (Malaysian Foreign Minister Ghazalie Shafie's phrase) is successfully implemented, the Government in Hanoi will get weakened and discredited. In such a situation, the pro-Chinese elements in Vietnam will revolt against the pro-Russian elements and a government friendly to China and amenable to Chinese interests will assume power in Hanoi.

Beijing successfully exploited ASEAN fears of Vietnam to the maximum. According to Kissinger, Deng undertook a journey to Southeast Asian countries and practiced his own brand of 'highly visible, blunt and occasionally hectoring diplomacy'. In November 1978, during his visit to Malaysia, Singapore and Thailand, Deng branded Vietnam as the 'Cuba 0f the East'. He pointed out that the security of Southeast Asia was threatened by the Soviet-Vietnamese Treaty. This Treaty 'is not directed against China alone...It is a very important world wide Soviet scheme. You may believe that the meaning of the Treaty is to encircle China. I have told friendly countries that China is not afraid of being encircled. It has a more important meaning for Asia and the Pacific. The security of Asia, the Pacific and the whole world are threatened'. The result was ASEAN, China and the US working together, and keeping the Heng Samrin Government out of the UN. The joint action implied legitimacy to the murderous Pol Pot regime. They also demanded the immediate withdrawal of Vietnamese troops from Kampuchea. China was then exhorting the Southeast Asian countries to exercise vigilance so that the 'tiger must be prevented from coming in from the backdoor while the wolf is repelled at the front gate'. But there was another danger which caused apprehension in the Indian minds. While driving the wolf out of the front door and warding off the Tiger through the backdoor, ASEAN should not allow the dragon to step in through the side door. In fact, the entire strategic significance of Indo-China revolved around that possibility. If Heng Samrin Government falls, China will be the next door neighbour of Thailand, with all its consequences. And if there was one country which could prevent such a possibility and stand up against the hegemonistic designs of Beijing, it was Vietnam.

Developments Within Indo-China

Kissinger turns a blind eye to the domestic developments within Indo-China, especially the emergence of the Pol Pot regime. As mentioned earlier, if one wants to understand the Third Indo-China War, one must clearly keep in mind the inter-related domestic and international developments.

After 1975, Vietnam subscribed to the view that after a protracted struggle against a common enemy, a new era of peace will usher in Indo-

China. Hanoi was keen to forge co-operative links with Kampuchea and Laos and proposed a 'special relationship', which implied joint utilisation of economic resources and co-operation in matters of defence like the stationing of Vietnamese troops in Laos. Kampuchea, as mentioned earlier, resented any mention of special relations, to them it smacked of Vietnamese hegemonistic designs.

In the new Kampuchea that the Khemer revolutionaries wanted to build, the Vietnamese had absolutely no place. As early as 1973, the Khemer Rouge had initiated a purge of pro-Vietnamese elements within the party. After the establishment of the revolutionary Government in 1975, the purge was continued and gathered momentum when Pol Pot assumed power in October 1976. Anti-Vietnamese sentiments were whipped up and thousands of Vietnamese had to flee for their lives. The Vietnam-Kampuchea border became tense and a series of border clashes took place in 1976 and 1977. Negotiations began in 1976, but could not make much headway due to the uncompromising stand of the Kampuchean Government. Gradually Kampuchea-Vietnam relations reached a point of no return. Vietnam began to openly advocate the overthrow of the Pol Pot Government.

By early 1978, the domestic politics of the Pol Pot government had affected large sections of the Khemer population. The crimes of the Pol Pot Government are well known and need not be narrated here. Conservative estimates of the number of people killed cross the two million mark, which does not include thousands who fled the country. In an interview with William Shawcross, Sihanouk said in 1977, "I lost two sons, two daughters, and ten grandchildren. I do not know whether they are dead, wounded or alive… I do not know what was happening in my country." To quote Sihanouk again, "In 1969, there were seven million Khemers. In 1979, there are less than four million Khemers in Kampuchea. According to UN estimates, in 1980 at least two million Khemers will die of famine or disease and also because of war, not to speak of the genocide that you know off." Pol Pot tried to gain maximum advantage of the conflict with Vietnam and projected himself as the saviour, defending the Khemer race against the historical enemy.

Till 1977, Hanoi was prepared to leave Kampuchea alone, even a strongly independent Kampuchea, so long as it did not play the

Chinese game. Pol Pot by himself was only a nuisance, but Pol Pot backed by China was a danger to Vietnam's survival. The Vietnamese believed with justification that the anti-Vietnamese stance of the Kampuchean Government was being fuelled and encouraged by China. In fact, the announcement that Kampuchea was under attack by Vietnam and its decision to sever diplomatic relations with Hanoi were made in Beijing. China extended whole hearted support to Kampuchea. On January 13, 1979, in a meeting with Ieng Sary, Hua Guofeng said, "The Kampuchean peoples struggle is our struggle. We supported you in the past, we are supporting you now and we will continue to support you in future." Hanoi considered Kampuchean attacks on Vietnam as indirect Chinese aggression. After repeated pronouncements describing the true nature, both internal and external of the Pol Pot regime, Vietnam resorted to the only course of action that was available. In December 1978, Vietnamese forces occupied Kampuchea and installed Heng Samrin in power.

Differences Within ASEAN

While Kissinger writes in glowing terms about the unity displayed by ASEAN, a keen student of Southeast Asian politics could discern subtle differences in the approach of the member states. The five countries differed in their own assessment of China and Vietnam, depending on their national interests and their appraisal of the geo-politics of the region and changing inter-relations among the super powers. Thailand, effectively backed by Singapore, was the most hawkish towards Vietnam in all ASEAN meetings and international forums. On the other hand, there was greater appreciation in Kuala Lumpur and Jakarta about Hanoi's fears and the factors that led to Vietnamese invasion of Kampuchea. The two countries wanted to find a political solution to the problem quickly, lest Vietnam gets destabilised in furtherance of Chinese strategy. They wanted Vietnam to be strong and independent and emerge as an independent centre of power, free from both Soviet Union and China. Sheldon Simon has summed up the intra-ASEAN differences as, "The primary disjunction in ASEAN lies between Thailand and Indonesia with Singapore aligning more with Bangkok, Malaysia leaning towards Indonesia, and the Philippines and Brunei located more or less in the middle."

Conclusion

Three decades after the end of the Third Indo-China War, the political landscape of Southeast and East Asia has completely changed. Pol Pot has become a frightful dream. Heng Samrin has consolidated his power by winning successive mandate from his people. Vietnam and China have normalised their relations, though the territorial disputes in the South China Sea continue to cast its long shadow. China has emerged as a political and economic giant and has become the major trading partner of all Southeast Asian countries. The US-China linkages have been strengthened although sections in the US are apprehensive of China's long term intentions and goals in Southeast Asia.

In retrospect, what impact did the Third Indo-China War have on political developments in Southeast Asia? First and foremost, it enabled the ASEAN to emerge as a united, cohesive and viable regional organisation. During its formative years ASEAN could neither influence regional developments nor bring about any change in the attitude of the super powers. The Third Indo-China War brought about a fundamental change. Prime Minister Phan Van Dong's visit to ASEAN capitals in 1978 could not make much headway. On the contrary, the member states of ASEAN rallied round the frontline state Thailand. Despite the differences in their perception of Vietnam and China, the regional organisation responded collectively and succeeded in rallying support to the ousted Pol Pot regime (despite its genocidal record) in the United Nations. ASEAN also demanded the withdrawal of Vietnamese forces from Cambodia as a precondition for a negotiated settlement. The author agrees with the assessment made by the Singapore scholar-diplomat Chang Heng Chee, "The Vietnamese occupation of Kampuchea was God sent. It became the common cause energizing the process of co-operation, galvanizing ASEAN unity. Without Kampuchea there was every likelihood that ASEAN would suffer internal dislocation on how to handle an emergent Vietnam and would be forced to confront the structuring of a long term strategy in a fluid environment."

Though it did not find vocal expression, the member states of ASEAN were not very happy that they were providing legitimacy to the ousted Pol Pot Government. Sihanouk, as quoted earlier, had severely criticised the policies of the Khemer Rouge Government. In Singapore, Sihanouk explicitly accused the Khemer Rouge of murdering his children and grand children and told how he himself was saved because of the intervention of his friend Chou En Lai. On another occasion, in New York, Sihanouk sought the US protection, denounced the Khemer Rouge for mass murder and called for their expulsion from the United Nations. On US' persuasion, Sihanouk eventually agreed to go to France. Singapore was conscious that the ASEAN policy was becoming more and more untenable. As Amb Nathan has written, "We did see a need to respond to the disastrous reputation that the Khemer Rouge was gaining internationally for the brutality and inhumanity of its regime." Nathan adds, "ASEAN's defence of the Khemer Rouge was becoming untenable, and equally it did not share China's desire to see the Khemer Rouge return to power after the Vietnamese withdrawal." Singapore began to work assiduously for an alternative, consisting of various nationalist elements in Cambodia. The Singapore Deputy Prime Minister Rajaratnam appealed to all freedom living Cambodians struggling against the Vietnamese Occupation to 'set aside their differences and come together in a new Cambodian united front and so present a new face to the international community'. Ieng Sary vehemently opposed the formation of a united front. Then Singapore played its trump card. If the proposal for a united front was not acceptable to Ieng Sary, Rajaratnam declared that 'he had no alternative but to instruct his delegate at the United Nations to vote for allowing the Vietnamese backed regime to take over the Cambodia seat in the UN'. The threat had its desired effect. Ieng Sary agreed that he would try to persuade the Khemer Rouge leaders to agree to the formation of a broad united front. Finally the three factions—led by Sihanouk, Son Sann and the Khemer Rouge respectively—issued a joint statement and announced that they would work together for forming a Coalition Government of Democratic Kampuchea.

A positive gain for Southeast Asian countries was China's decision to terminate its powerful ideological support to the communist parties. The situation was rendered complex by the fact that in Malaysia and Singapore, the revolutionary leadership and militant following of the communist parties came from ethnic Chinese. It may be recalled that even when PRC established diplomatic relations with member states of ASEAN, beginning with Malaysia in 1974, it maintained the distinction between party-to-party relations and government-to-government relations. Lee Kuan Yew in the course of his visits to China explained that this policy was acting as a hindrance in the normalisation of China's relations with Southeast Asian countries. To quote Lee, "There are underlying suspicions and animosity between the Malay Muslims and Chinese in Malaysia and between Indonesians and the ethnic Chinese." Because China was exporting revolution to Southeast Asia, many ASEAN neighbours were reluctant to side with China against the Soviet Union. They regarded radio broadcasts from China appealing directly to ethnic Chinese as 'dangerous subversion'. Lee Kuan Yew's persuasive diplomacy had its desired effect. China wound up the broadcasting stations operating from Southern China.

In his book, Kissinger quotes Lee Kuan Yew to suggest that the Third Indo-China War prevented the fall of dominoes to Vietnamese supported communist parties. To quote Kissinger, "Singapore's Prime Minister Lee Kuan Yew has summed up the ultimate result of the war: The Western press wrote off the Chinese punitive action as a failure. I believe it changed the history of East Asia." A question naturally comes to the Indian minds— were the Southeast Asian countries in the late 1970s weaklings to fall like dominoes before Vietnamese onslaught? I believe that by the late 1970s, the Southeast Asian countries, including Singapore, had developed sufficient resilience to withstand both internal and external pressures.

7

Kissinger's Views on US-China Economic Relations

K. Subramanian

In his book *On China,* Dr. Henry Kissinger had a vision of the future of US-China economic relations. Indeed, it is very tempting, coming as it does, from a diplomat who was a cold realist all along his life, and who did not hesitate to take unconventional or contrarian views on many issues. Naturally, the book is all about America's relations with Beijing.

The present is a time where neither the US faces important external challenges nor is it likely to face in the foreseeable future. Therefore, as Kissinger notes, "The relationship between China and the United States has become a central element in the quest for world peace and global well-being."

As a part of this quest, Kissinger articulates a vision of a 'Pacific Community', which he describes as 'a region to which the United States, China and other states all belong and in whose peaceful development all participate'. The concept has its historical parallel in the Atlantic Community formed after the Second World War. Further, he feels that the emergence of a Pacific community would 'reflect the reality that the US is an Asian power' and also respond to 'China's aspiration to a global role'. Indeed, by this argument, he tries to hold a balance between the current strategic expectations or goals of the US and the claims (demands!) of emerging nationalist Chinese.

Kissinger may not be accused of being a utopian in his assessment. He is cautious and tentative, and his hopes for the future of Sino-American relations are 'more about what should not happen than what should happen'. These are based on the current template of relations between the two countries and the seeds of tensions and potential conflicts. What are the conflicts?

The contentious issues read more like a laundry list and to summarise selectively are Currency rate for Yuan; Financial and market opening by China; WTO issue such as those on subsidies and the non-market status for China; China's Innovation policy which causes consternation among MNC investors; IPR issues; Standards policy of China which tends to restrict trade volumes with MNCs; Public procurement policy; supply chain maintenance; hurdles to Chinese investment in the US, especially by its sovereign wealth funds and China's Rare Earth Elements policy. Each issue has its historical baggage and newer developments complicate them by the day. And yet, negotiations are ongoing in various forums, especially in the Strategic and Economic Dialogue (S&ED). These do not include security or strategic issues like China's South Sea forays, its naval expansion to safeguard transportation of oil and raw material, its footprints in Africa and Latin America. These strategic issues stemming from the rapid growth of China get surcharged, and create the potential for clashes.

In the background of these conflicts, actual or potential, Kissinger's first fear is that the relations between the two countries should not degenerate into a zero-sum game. He devotes pages to analyse what happens when great nations compete without inhibitions. The rise of Germany after its unification unsettled the European balance and led inevitably to war. Though he notes that 'even the most precise analogy does not oblige the present generation to repeat the mistakes of its predecessors', he is uneasy about the postures of the US and China.

Many foreign policy analysts believe that the conflicts between the US and China are real but they will not necessarily turn into war. "Most scholars agree that the conflict between the two countries include their political incompatibility, economic competition, and military competition, but there are disagreements on what is the fundamental conflict between the two countries."[1]

Many neo-conservative analysts' 'regime change', including issues like 'democracy', 'human rights', etc. (the usual bandwagon!) become dominant and create excessive heat and rhetoric. Kissinger does not share this view and feels that Washington should not seek to change the nature of the Chinese state. This flows from his deep reading of China's history and his relations with Chinese leaders and the public over the last forty years. He has undertaken more than seventy trips to China and some of them were personal. The only other person who can make a similar claim is Hank Paulson, the former US Treasury Secretary.

He wonders whether the US will be able to change the Chinese political (state) structure or is ready to pay the price for such a regime change. Though Kissinger does not mention it, the US misadventures in Iraq and Afghanistan should inform future policy makers. He goes along with the view that while dealing with the Chinese leaders, other countries should recognise that China's policies on national security, including economic security, are strongly influenced by 'China's formative and developmental experience, particularly its negative treatment at the hands of the members of the international community, China's exploitation by other states during the 'century of shame' from the mid-1840s to the time of the establishment5 of the People's Republic in 1949'.[2]

In short, some of these issues are sensitive and create sharp reactions from the Chinese authorities. It is also significant that, perhaps for the same reasons such as his deep understanding of the Chinese polity, its psyche and the attitudes of its leaders, he does not condemn the Chinese over their suppression at Tiananmen Square, as many US analysts habitually tend to do. He pleads for a combination of 'realism' and 'idealism' in dealing with future relations with the Chinese to ensure the 'best outcome.'

Indeed, he is not dreamy-eyed about a Pacific Community or 'a partnership' between Washington and Beijing. A more likely development is what he calls 'co-evolution,' which means that 'both countries pursue their domestic imperatives, cooperating where possible, and adjust their relations to minimise conflict'. This implies that the two sides should 'attempt to elevate familiar crisis discussions into a more comprehensive framework that eliminates the underlying causes of the tensions'. There are many as listed earlier.

This takes us on to the issues of economic interdependence and the changes in their relationships. The changes have come about partly in response to developments and mostly in the growing interaction between the US and China, which had become the dominant economic powers.

Economists like Niall Ferguson could coin pithy names like 'Chimerica' to describe the newer relations.

China, which was isolated and shut out from the global trading system in the 1950s and 1960s, has turned into the second most important power. The estimates of the IMF suggest that it will overtake the US by 2016. As Arvind Subramanian put it,[3] "When the presidents of China and the United States met last week in Washington, neither was likely to be aware that measured in terms of purchasing power, it is Hu Jintao, and not Barack Obama, who represented the world's largest economy."

For years, the American public had viewed China as a poor developing country which was rising due to the helpful hand extended by the US in the post Nixon years. During the cold war years, it was one of 'engagement.' Indeed, China was transforming and emerging as a member of the international community. China could enter many international organisations including the World Trade Organization (WTO). It was the assurance of access to US market that led to economic reforms and catalysed China's attempts to modernise its economy. The export-oriented development was based on the new found relationship with the US It led to large flows of foreign direct investment and a greater role for US companies to enter the Chinese market and create export platforms, supply chains, etc. which began to feed the western mills. It was truly a part of the new wave of globalisation and the ascendancy of the Washington Consensus as a philosophy of economic development.

It has to be noted that in all its efforts, unlike many developing countries including India, China did not depend on western or American assistance for its development. It has given them policy autonomy to decide issues based on national priorities and not on terms set by others. They drew upon their own national savings and directed state-owned banks (all banks were state-owned in the early years!) to fund the construction of massive infrastructure which has made China the envy of all developing countries and turned that country into a hub of global manufacturing. This is not the place to describe the phenomenon of 'China price', which attracts most MNCs to set up shop in China. There is a premium of at least 30 to 40 per cent when companies produce in China.

Moreover, China is obsessively concerned about 'comprehensive economic security' for the country and its people. They continue to rely on state-owned enterprises to enhance productive capabilities and assure employment to the labour force.

Their policy governing the exchange rate for their currency Yuan is holistic, and seeks to preserve economic and social stability. This is not appreciated by the US or other governments in their disputes with China.

We refer to these to establish the hypothesis that differences in perception between China and other governments often lead to misapprehensions. In a rare interview, Kissinger[4] explained the decision making process in China. He said, "American business leaders tend to think of their activities as a series of episodes to be managed by legal process and predictable norms. The Chinese manage their internal affairs by relationships, not by processes. So when one operates in China, one has to understand how the social and cultural network operates." He went on to elaborate how 'the Chinese managed to keep their internal decision-making process untransparent for centuries'. He expressed the hope that the process would become more transparent as it evolves.

Unfortunately, an average citizen in the US does not have the experience or prescience of Kissinger, and is given to irrational fears. It is an area where economic interdependence creates misgivings. Even by 2007, a Report[5] of an Independent Task Force sponsored by the Council on Foreign Relations detailed the sources of unease governing US China relations. It noted, "China's rapid economic development, accompanied by an enormous and growing trade surplus with the US tates, is a major factor. The economic challenge posed by China has become synonymous with the larger challenge of globalisation, especially the pressures created by competition with low-wage economies." Trade deficit is estimated at US$ 270 billion during 2011 and has gone on unabated since 2003-04. That is not the only part.

The other part is the growing debt of the US which rose to US$ 14 trillion in 2010 and is expected to cross US$ 15 trillion this year. At the same time, China has built a foreign exchange reserve of over US$ 3.4 trillion and has invested around 60 to 70 per cent of it in US Treasuries or Agency papers. The financial crisis has put paid to the claims of the superiority of the US style capitalist model vis-a-vis the Chinese. The Standard and Poor (S&P) downgrade of US Treasuries was a psychological blow to the Americans. There are fears on both sides—the fear on the US's side that the Chinese could pull out the Treasuries and bring down the dollar; the fear of the Chinese that US' monetary policies, in particular Quantitative Easing could destroy the value of their assets. In fact, the current economic crisis seems to have led to a new relationship – one of 'balanced terror' as in the cold war era. Fortunately, both sides are restrained by their assessment that victory, if any, would be pyrrhic.

American people increasingly feel that China is catching up to the US According to a survey conducted by the Washington-based Pew Research Center for the People and the Press in 2011, about 47 per cent of participants say China, not the US, is the world's top economic power, while 31 per cent continue to name the US Though the survey does not fully suggest ground realities, it reflects that American people feel anxious with China's growing power and influence. There is a fear among US officials of losing global influence compared to China. President Obama had to declare repeatedly that the US would remain the number one economic power.

The fear of becoming or remaining a 'declining power' could affect policies and global strategies. As one of the *Financial Times* columnists explained,[6] "America must manage its decline." Even if American analysts deny the reality of its declining status, it may influence their policies in an unintended way.

As explained by Zhou,[7] realists believe that the relationship between the two will basically be stable and peaceful. However, pessimists suggest that 'rising states usually want to translate their power into greater authority in the global system in order to stand up by taking assertive strategy toward the US In fact, they begin to wonder whether China is departing from Deng Xiaoping's foreign policy of *tao guang yang hui* (hide brightness and cherish obscurity) towards the US Elizabeth Economy of the Council on Foreign Relations wonders whether the consensus of the Deng era has begun to fray, and Beijing has begun to expand its influence to the rest of the world.

There are sober analysts who see current trends differently. Joseph Nye Jr. presented[8] a different perspective. Referring to asymmetries in economic interdepence, which limit the powers of the partners, and to the formation of Groups like G-20 to share power, he takes this view, "Neither side is in a hurry to break the asymmetry of their vulnerability interdependence, but each side continues to jockey to shape the structure and institutional framework of their market relationship."

Prof. Boutin of Deakin University takes a more realistic view[9] on the current situation. He adds, "The common ground is eroding the most where the United States is concerned. The greater salience of national economic security means that regional economic and political trends are having the greatest impact in this case. American authorities are experiencing the greatest difficulties accommodating their national and comprehensive economic security objectives, and are likely to be faced with increasingly difficult choices. For the present, they are responding by limiting transnational collaboration by American industry in key sectors. A strengthening of this tendency has considerable potential to undermine the extensive economic interdependence which has developed in the Chinese and American economies, with a negative impact on comprehensive economic security in both the cases."

Needless to add, both the countries have much to gain by greater cooperation. Unfortunately, they are caught in a trap. As Nye Jr. puts it,[10] "..... hubris and nationalism among some Chinese as well as unnecessary fear of decline among some Americans make it difficult to assure this future."

Economic interdependence need not necessarily bring about greater welfare among countries. They could create tensions, loss of trade, investment, etc. Policymakers should learn to manage or direct the relations to serve agreed priorities. On date, such an agreement on priorities is lacking and Kissinger's vision of a Pacific Community is wishful.

Notes

1. Jinghao Zhou, American Perspectives versus Chinese Expectations on China's Rise, International Journal of China Studies, vol. 2, no. 3, December 2011, pp. 625-645.
2. Kenneth J.D. Boutin, Beyond Interdependence: The Challenge of Economic Security in a Changing Political and Economic Landscape, Deakin University, 2011. www.deakin.edu.au/arts-ed/shss/events/fulbright/boutin.pdf

3. Arvind Subramanian, Is China already Number One? New GDP estimates, East Asia
     Forum, 2011. http://www.eastasiaforum.org/2011/02/03/is-china-already-number-one-
     new-gdp-estimates

4. Henry Kissinger, China Then and Now. http:/finance.fortune.cnn.com/2011/09/08/
     henry-kssinger-china-the-and-now/

5. US-China Relations: An Affirmative Agenda, A Responsible Course, Report of an
     Independent Task Force, Council on Foreign Relations, 2007.

6. Gideon Rachman, America must manage its Decline, *Financial Times*, October 17,
     2011.

7. Ibid., n. 1.

8. Joseph Nye, American and Chinese Power after the Financial Crisis, *The Washington
     Quarterly*, October 2010.

9. Ibid., n. 2.

10. Ibid., n. 8.

8

Re-Evaluating US Policy Towards Asia

Saurabh Kumar

It is a privilege to be asked to conclude our deliberations at this seminar on '*Re-evaluating US Foreign Policy towards Asia*'—Eastern Asia (and the Asia-Pacific region) essentially, I take it, going by the structure of the sessions. I would like to thank the organisers for this honour and for inviting me to participate in this very well-conceived conference on a theme that is of obvious interest to the international affairs confraternity in our country. It clearly needs to be examined in depth for it is of utmost importance that we gauge the import of what appears to be a new US approach towards the Asia-Pacific region correctly. This discussion, the first of its kind to my knowledge, is therefore timely and the initiative of the University of Madras, the Centre for Asia Studies and the Chennai Centre for China Studies, deserving of compliments.

Kissinger's latest book 'On China', which the Concept Note of the seminar has highlighted, provides a useful backdrop to any analysis of US foreign policy in Asia—for China obviously holds the key to understanding the US approach to Asia (and much of the world) today. The China-US bilateral equation is by far the most important determinant of the fabric of contemporary international relations—'one of the most challenging and consequential bilateral relationships the US has ever had to manage', in the words of US Secretary of State, Ms. Hillary Clinton—making it a better take-off point for delving into the multiple feedback loops in international affairs than any other. And what better source for laying the inter-connections of this minefield bare than the *weltanschauung*, and experience of one of the most consummate practitioners of strategic diplomacy and perhaps the foremost interlocutor the Chinese may have ever had. Except for the fact, which should in my opinion be borne in mind with due respect to the prodigious reputation of the man, that these are his projections for the consumption of others, and not necessarily the truth, or even his true thoughts or feelings about the events, issues, and individuals on the stage of history. An obvious point, that applies to all authors without exception actually—and not to Kissinger alone.

This note of caution might not have been necessary—not, at any hand, to an enlightened and expert audience such as the present one—but bears mention perhaps in the light of the somewhat simplistic manner, in my opinion, in which disclosures emanating from Wikileaks have often been treated in the media in the country and in the public discourse (including sometimes at political levels, it has to be said)—as if the actors involved (in the Wikileaks revelations) had the same vantage point as ours or were entirely disinterested parties, with no angles or agendas of their own to advance.

I am no expert on US foreign policy, and am therefore not qualified to critique Kissinger's take on historical developments. But one cannot help suspecting a certain 'tweaking', if one could take the liberty of putting it that way, of the motivations underlying the actions of different actors at crucial junctures in history—at least when it comes to the US role. Deflecting attention away from US motivations appears to be a Kissingerian forte. One is left wondering if some of the conceptually complex and complicated formulations proffered by him at a number of places in the book are not a clever contrivance to gloss over US compulsions, constraints or plain helplessness—a way of making a virtue out of necessity, to put it simply. I hope historians in the country would let us have the benefit of their considered assessment of the correctness and veracity of his interpretations, which the book advances with the benefit of hindsight (i.e. not as a running commentary, as is sometimes mistakenly treated), based on their independent study of international developments in the post-Second World War era.

Moving to the contemporary scene, the theme of the seminar, there would perhaps be little justification for making an omnibus survey of the same ground after a full day's exchange of views. So, I will try and confine myself to some remarks that seem to me to be pertinent for a 'reevaluation' of the US policy and strategy on overall considerations, and to some questions that came to mind in that perspective, in the relatively short notice given to me. Before doing so, let us just take stock of what we know about the content of the (new) US approach towards Eastern Asia and the Asia-Pacific—as observers constrained to base themselves on secondary sources openly available in the academic world. We have gone over it in detail in earlier sessions; so, only a bare outline in these few slides for ready recall.

Slide 1

I. *Articulation of a new strategic policy posture by the US:*

    a. US Secretary of State Clinton's article in' Foreign Policy' of Oct 2011

    b. US President Obama's speeches during his November 2011 tour of some Asia-Pacific countries and at the East Asia and APEC Summits

    c. A host of other articulations from the US academia on cue in the ensuing weeks

The noted US scholar, Kenneth Lieberthal, has summarised the essence of these articulations in the following terms:

> *(It is an)* "*an integrated diplomatic, military, and economic strategy that stretches from the Indian subcontinent through Northeast Asia", with the core message that "America is going to play a leadership role in Asia for decades to come.*"

Slide 2

II. *Antecedents and other Actions accompanying articulation of the new policy posture:*

    a. US Secretary of State, Clinton's statement at the Hanoi ASEAN Regional Forum (ARF) in July 2010 (and US Defence Secretary Gates' presentation at the Shangri La dialogue in June that year), which categorically declared US 'national interest' in:

        • *'freedom of navigation in ...Asia's maritime commons' and 'respect for international law in the South China Sea'.*

- '*(all claimants) resolving the various territorial disputes without coercion', and opposition to 'the use or threat of use of force by any claimant'.*
- '*resolution of claims (and accompanying rights in maritime space) in accordance with UNCLOS' and 'derived solely from legitimate claims to land features'.*
- *(ARF parties reaching) 'agreement on a full Code of Conduct', with reference to the long standing deliberations on the issue, which have made little progress (beyond a toothless Declaration of 2002, and Guidelines for its Implementation finally agreed upon in 2011) due to Chinese stalling and preference for addressing the disputes bilaterally, and not multilaterally.*

[This would have been coordinated, in advance obviously, with Vietnam—the Chair—and the 10 other members of the ARF who raised the South China Sea issue on the

occasion.]

Slide 3

b. *Series of steps taken by the US in 2010 and 2011 in response to aggressive Chinese actions at the diplomatic and military levels since 2009 (particularly after Assistant Foreign Minister Cui Tiankai reportedly told Assistant Secretary Kurt Campbell, during his visit in March 2010, that the South China Sea islands in dispute were amongst China's 'core interests'):*

  i.   *South Korea: Finalising of KORUS, the Korea-US Free Trade Agreement; large scale joint exercises with it in the Sea of Japan and the Yellow Sea, following North Korea's sinking of Republic of Korea's (ROK) ship Cheonan and other provocations—against Chinese objections. (July-September 2010)*

  ii. *Japan: Support to Japan over the fishing boat incident by affirming that the US-Japan Treaty covers the Senkaku waters. (September 2010)*

iii. *Taiwan: Pressing ahead with the US$ 6 billion arms aid package to Taiwan overriding Chinese objections. (September 2010)*

iv. *East Asia Summit (EAS): Losing no time in making its presence felt (in the EAS in its maiden participation in November 2011) by putting the new forum (for it) to use to focus on difficult maritime security issues, reiterating US interest in a 'principles based' approach to maritime security outlined by Clinton at the Hanoi ARF in July 2010. (November 2011)*

[This was in contrast to the leisurely pace of discussion in the ARF (which is, for that very reason, China's preferred forum—albeit under cover of professing to espouse the 'ASEAN way', playing upon the desire of ASEAN countries to keep it ASEAN driven).]

v. *APEC: Advancing the 'Trans-Pacific Partnership' (TPP)—a 'WTO plus' trade and investment platform based on principles potentially unwelcome to China (transparency, labour rights, TPP, environmental standards, etc.), with a view to ensuring its exclusion obviously. (November 2011)*

[The TPP is not yet a reality (but targeted to be made so soon, possibly in 2012 itself, under this push by the US as the Chair)—so the impact of this step remains to be seen. The US is obviously seeking to reverse the asymmetry of its not being a member of the PRC-ASEAN FTA and being left outside the fold of the ASEAN+3 (China, Japan, and ROK) cooperation.]

vi. *Japan: Beefing up the US-Japan Treaty, encouraging Japan to enlarge its defence perimeter and role of its military, and move towards trilateral US Japan-ROK coordination (besides dropping its earlier resistance to the idea of Japan joining the TPP).*

vii. *Australia: Agreement providing, inter alia, for deployment of up to 2,500 marines (in Darwin, closer to the South China Sea islands than other US bases in the region), with plans for expansion of US-Australia defence ties 'from a Pacific partnership to an Indo-*

*Pacific one' and integration of the Western Pacific and Indian
Ocean naval activities.*

viii. *The Philippines, Thailand, and Vietnam: Strengthening military,
and overall, ties not just with the Philippines, Thailand but also with
Vietnam (including joint exercises and training; visit of a destroyer
and transit of an aircraft carrier in August 2010, immediately after
the Hanoi ARF amidst open Vietnamese-Chinese spats over the
Paracel islands; commencement of cooperation in the sensitive
nuclear area, etc.).*

ix. *Myanmar: Working out a surprise new opening towards Myanmar
after long years of boycott that had driven it into the arms of China.*

x.   *India: Strengthening of relations with India (and encouraging loose
talk amongst the chatterati of its role as a 'balancer' to Chinese
preponderance in the S.E. and East Asian region).*

The US initiatives over the past year formed a pattern more clearly.
Kenneth Lieberthal describes it as follows:

Slide 4
*"......whereas previously the US selectively pushed back............and
focused great attention on managing the overall US-China relationship, the
November 2011 trip (of Obama) marked a significant shift.*
*Washington is still very much focused on sustaining a constructive US-
China relationship, but it has now brought disparate elements together in
a strategically integrated fashion that explicitly affirms and promises to
sustain American leadership throughout Asia for the foreseeable future."*
(emphasis added)

So we have these two-tiered tell-tale signs of the content of the new US
policy approach to go by as signposts in our endeavour to understand what
is going on—first the explicit (and high level) articulation of the last few
months, and secondly, the same strategic approach (as in the articulation)
implicit in the actions already begun to be taken more than a year earlier in
2010, that is, the Articulation, on the one hand, and the Actions, on the other.

We need to reflect on both of them in order to be able to assess the import of the new US policy and posture correctly.

The question that arises, to my mind, is why the walk should have preceded the talk, in a reversal of the usual order of precedence—of actions on the ground following the formulation and articulation of grand strategy? There was no talk of a new policy approach of 'pivoting towards Asia' or whatever in 2010 (or even in the first half of 2011) when fairly definitive and considered responses were being made, and political signals conveyed to the Chinese by the Americans in no uncertain terms and in abundant measure. So, one is naturally led to wonder what is the trigger for the high profile launch of this new strategic posture in the last quarter of 2011? We clearly need to understand that if we are to be able to contextualise the policy pronouncements and actions correctly, that is, to understand where they (the Americans) are coming from, if we are to understand correctly where they are headed to and, consequently, what lies ahead for others in the region?

This is obviously not easy because we are not privy to all that is going on between the Chinese and the Americans, especially between their militaries. But the question has to be asked, and an answer attempted, howsoever tentatively. One important development that might possibly hold a clue, I would like to suggest, is the significant enhancement in the Chinese technical infrastructure supporting its military potential, in the US perception, sometime towards the end of 2010 as a result of a number of developments that were underway, and maturing, around that time; above all, the attainment of ASBM Initial Operating Capability (IOC), which was disclosed to the rest of the world by Admiral Willard of the US Pacific Command in December 2010, and which may hold the key to the mystery.

[A word about the significance of ASBM capability, which would be appreciated by all I am sure. It is acknowledged to be a game-changer, providing a counter (to force projection through aircraft carrier led battle groups) where none existed, by creating uncertainty on the American side about their capacity to ensure safe and secure passage of their battle group—with all the attendant adverse impact on their prestige that an ASBM blow to their advancing aircraft carrier group is capable of causing. As such, it has a crucial bearing on the Chinese capacity to challenge the hitherto unassailable US supremacy over the seas in their neighbourhood and beyond, all the way up to the second island chain in the Western Pacific—if not further. Not surprisingly, the Anti-Ship Ballistic Missile (ASBM) is being seen in the US as the ultimate 'asymmetric equaliser' in China's armoury and warfare strategy seeking to level up disadvantage vis-a-vis a superior adversary by such clever ancient stratagems, ducking a head on, parity seeking, arms race.

I share this assessment with confidence, without any naval expertise, on the strength of a recently completed NIAS project on the ASBM initiated by Admiral Ganesh (Retd).]

There are other aspects of enhancement of Chinese naval and overall military potential (that matured or came to light not long after, in 2011 but which would have been known (to the US) to be under development and maturing, and therefore, might have been contributory factors to the new US strategic posture), apart from the ASBM:

Slide 5
- *5th generation Stealth fighter aircraft, J-20 (revealed during the Gates visit (July 2011)*
- *Increasing frequency of cyber attacks demonstrated in an unremitting series of hacking incidents*
- *Stepped up space activities—22 satellites from 19 launches, higher than the US' 18 launches and second only to Russia's 36, as well as the successful docking of the Shenzhou module with the space station, Tiangong and successful operationalisation of the satellite navigation system, Beidou—and the notice of mega space ambitions served in the new Space Plan announced at the end of 2010*
- *Trial sailing of China's first aircraft carrier*
- *Test launching of SLBMs in January 2012 (signifying overcoming of operationalisation difficulties)*

The access denial capability afforded to the Chinese by the ASBM would in itself have been a nightmare for the US, used to unquestioned sway over the global high seas; in conjunction with these other facets and technologies capable of lending a cutting edge to China's politico-military strategic posture and strategy, it might perhaps have been reckoned as just too much (of a synergistic build up) to be left unresponded to.

The timing of this development—coming as it did towards the end of 2010, after the 'action-reaction' cycle witnessed in 2009-10 and highlighted in the slides (over-confidence driven rashness, on the Chinese side, and alarm induced reactive measures on the US side) had played themselves out—fits in pretty well with the timing of the US policy announcement in October-November, nine months after the ASBM, Initial Operational Capability (IOC), and just a few months after unveiling of the J-20 Stealth fighter aircraft. As such, it (the ASBM IOC and associated military/technological attainments) would seem to qualify as a candidate for the policy trigger, or driver, that we are searching for.

Of course, there could be other possible, non-military and even non-bilateral, drivers of the new US strategic posture—realisation of heavy US dependence on the region for recovery of its economy (exports to Asian markets for growth, purchase of US Treasury bonds for maintenance of financial stability—including by China itself, and so on); need to close in the political space gradually opening up for China to draw the economies of the region into its economic orbit (as e.g. by gradually advancing its currency as an international reserve through currency swap arrangements); need to bolster the waning confidence of allies in the wake of growing Chinese gall. Each of these would, therefore, need to be examined and evaluated for their salience and significance for the task at hand. I would submit, however, that while they may all be contributory factors, they do not somehow fit the bill as immediate drivers of the new US posture the way the ASBM and associated military developments do.

Why is the question of trigger/driver important? Because it can help in throwing some light on what the motivation for US public pronouncement of the new policy approach of 2011 might be. If Chinese ASBM capability (and other related naval and strategic deterrent capabilities) were the (or even the primary) driver, the motivation—if it can be surmised without much strain—would be to try and box the Chinese back into the confines of the continental landmass they were seeking to break out of (towards the high seas) on the strength of the ASBM and other advancements In other words, 'containment'—that grand strategy that had delivered so well in case of the original challenger, the Soviet Union.

Not surprisingly, most Chinese analysts have viewed it to be so (though, notably, China has stopped short of taking that position officially yet). So also those independent observers, who are not constrained by the burdens of office in recognising realpolitik when they see it. The fact that such an objective has been denied by the US side explicitly, at various levels on a number of occasions, does not alter this inference in the least since the denials all have something to do with a Chinese audience looking over the speaker's shoulder, literally or a step or two removed.

Government spokesmen can, in any case, hardly be expected to do otherwise when confronted with a direct question of this kind point blank. Likewise, for the pious positive sentiments about the US welcoming a strong and prosperous China playing a greater role in the region, etc. expressed *ad nauseum* in official documents signed between the two countries.

Of course, not containment of the kind that was applied to the Soviet Union, openly, in defence against an ideologically aggressive Communist camp of the time threatening to take over the entire capitalist world in due course—which it would obviously not be reasonable to contemplate today—but 'covert containment' carried out by indirect means, as suited to and feasible in a globalised, intensely inter-connected world. One that will naturally be that much more difficult, and complicated, to execute with the US committed, for the record, *inter alia* to 'building a positive, cooperative, and comprehensive relationship for the 21st century' (with China). Hence, perhaps the (fine) distinction sought to be made in literature between containment and 'countervailing power', even though the two are the same in essence—especially when the latter is brought to bear in a concerted manner, in coordination with allies.

Needless to say—as with individuals, so with nations in some ways—it is impossible to pronounce with certainty what the motivation for a particular action might be, and one can only attempt (hazard might be a more appropriate word here) a guess. The possibility of being off the mark can not, therefore, be ruled out ever. It may well be that the main trigger was not military but diplomatic; simply the desire to cash in on the apprehensions its allies in the region have about growing Chinese power. Even so, the rationalisation (of the new US policy approach of pivoting towards Asia) advanced on the US side, and dutifully repeated in much of the discussion on strategic forums on the I-net—namely, that the wars in Iraq and Afghanistan having drawn, or drawing, to a close, the US is now free to turn its diplomatic, economic and military assets, attention and energies to the Asia-Pacific theatre (whose geo-political importance for the US is not denied but not accorded its due weight either, in comparison to its geoeconomic importance which is played up in a bid to underplay the extent of inter-twining of the two)—is not very convincing, to my mind. Self-evident at one (descriptive) level, I find it to be lacking in explanatory power. It sounds more like an after thought aimed at concealing, or fighting shy of admitting, the real trigger of the policy shift (that is euphemistically being described as 'pivoting towards Asia' but which, in reality, is very likely to amount to nothing short of a policy of containment). Even the rush for a Trans-Pacific Partnership, with Japan in it after years of lack of interest in its inclusion, makes sense only in this perspective—of being seen as an instrument for containment, because of its bringing in extra-economic standards, not as a trade promotion measure, as the eminent economist, Jagdish Bhagwati (otherwise well disposed towards US foreign policy), has pointed out in no uncertain terms.

This is also clear from the latest US Defence Strategic Review entitled *'Sustaining US Global Leadership: Priorities for 21st Century Defence'*, personally released by Obama on January 05, 2012, which proposes a renewed stress on the Asia-Pacific region through a 'rebalancing (of forces) towards the East'. Though it naturally does not name China as the adversary, that is amply evident from its very architecture and from the thinly veiled allusions in its declaration of determination to deal with the threat posed by enemies that would use ballistic missiles or other 'asymmetric means' to ward off US forces and inclusion of 'anti-access and area denial' capability in the Pacific amongst its priority missions.

The former Singapore Prime Minister, Lee Kuan Yew, one of the most astute observers of the Chinese and global scene known to speak his mind without exaggeration or hyperbole, put it in crystal clear terms when he spoke of 2010 as marking the beginning of a 'decade long tussle between the US and China for pre-eminence in the Pacific'. Likewise, a by-no-means pro-Chinese commentator like Gideon Rachman (whose October 04, 2011 article in the Financial Times was commended by Subramaniam in his remarks for the light it shed on the state of play between China and the US), and a host of others with a keen eye on developments in the region and unafraid to call a spade a spade.

If that be the case, that is, if the name of the game is going to be confrontation and contention—under whatever label and of whatever hue— then the following questions taken from the Abstract of an article in the latest issue of the American journal, Foreign Affairs, should be of interest to us in India too.

Slide 6
Will an era of the US-Chinese tension be as dangerous as the Cold War? Or less because of their intense inter-connectedness? Or will it be even worse because China, unlike the Soviet Union, is likely to prove to be a serious economic competitor for the US, besides a geopolitical one?

We should be pondering, in other words, over the fallout of a US policy of 'containment in all but name' on others in the region, on ourselves above all, given the extreme sensitivity of the India-China relationship—which, it bears remembering, is *sui generis*—to its larger, external, environment. This is a point that should need no elaboration to this cognoscenti gathering. Not, at any hand, after the dip on this front witnessed in the second half of the last decade, just as most observers in the country—many seasoned China hands included—thought the border negotiations had finally been put on 'delivery mode' (reflected in their ready consecration of the relationship into a 'strategic' partnership, without substantive basis to warrant that honorific, on successful conclusion of the first phase of the negotiations—in anticipation of forward movement, obviously, in the next phase), so I shall say no more here.

The next question that again flows from the first one (pointing to containment as the unstated rationale for the 'pivoting' proclamation) is about feasibility. Some US scholars (mainstream ones, not ill-disposed to the Obama Administration) have wondered if this is a realistic approach, that is, does America have the resources to make good on a policy of containment ('make good on this rhetoric' are the words used by Lieberthal) at a time when there is a huge question mark over its own, European and the world economies? At a time of soaring deficits (40% of its budget) and consequent potential defence budget (which constitutes 20% of US federal budget) cuts of US$ 1 trillion over the next decade, as against the double digit increases the Chinese defence budget is set to enjoy (if extrapolations of existing trends hold).

[Digression: The US defence budget will grow, not decrease, despite US$ 489 billion cuts proposed by Obama in the DSR over the next 10 years; only not as fast as hitherto. Additional cuts of US$ 600 billion are expected to kick in as a result of failure to reach agreement in the US Congress to reduce the deficit as part of the August debt ceiling deal.]

US Defence Secretary Gates had admitted as much at the Singapore Shangri La Dialogue in June 2010, "Sustaining this forward military presence and commitments is costly, and cannot be disentangled from the wider discussion of the US fiscal predicament in general."

Of course, Obama unequivocally declared during his November 2011 travel that Asian security investments would be protected from future cuts in overall US defence spending and he has re-iterated that message while releasing the Defence Strategy Review last week. And the Republicans, dead set though they may be against big Government, are not against big Defence budgets as Paul Krugman points out time and again, so Obama's assurance may not be upturned in the event of a Republican Presidency post-2012 but, intentions and subjective desires apart, the question of feasibility will not go away. The lessons of US over-extension in the post Cold War period are being recalled as something the US can ignore only at its peril. These arguments and doubts are bound to surface more prominently, and fall into sharper relief, as nitty-gritty matters of detail come to occupy centre stage in the US discourse in due course.

Likewise, the question of political will (to sustain a strategy of containment), the resource constraint aside, is also pertinent. In the words of

Lieberthal again, an expert not unsympathetic to the objectives of the policy, it is 'easier said than done'. The US needs China's cooperation on several critical problem areas—the Iranian and the DPRK nuclear proliferation imbroglios, above all—not to mention global (economic) governance issues. This raises serous doubts about US inclination and capacity to exert itself to do all it would take to check China.

It may be noted here that, amongst the numerous 'dialogues' between the two countries, is one specifically on the Asia-Pacific. Two rounds have been held so far, both in 2011 (in June and October), just when the containment approach must have been in the making! South Asia was amongst the subjects discussed, at least in the second round, according to a US Press Release on the occasion; so, Indian analysts cannot but wonder what to make of US intentions.

It is not clear, of course, what is meant by the allusion to 'South Asia'— the situation in Afghanistan or the older connotation, whereby the US and China used to confabulate on India and Pakistan (which has been taken, in Indian strategic circles, to have ended after the strong reaction in India to such mention in the 2009 US-China Joint Statement issued at the end of Obama's maiden visit to China). In this connection, a sentence from Clinton's article in 'Foreign Policy' merits greater attention than it seems to have received in the country: ".....we are setting our sights as well on enhancing coordination and engagement among the three giants of the Asia-Pacific—China, India and the US."

Because of the heavy inter-dependence and inter-connectedness of all the economies of the region—and that is the case not just with those of China and the US but also other bilateral of China, that is, Japan, ROK, ASEAN, Taiwan, etc.—there are severe limits to the extent to which a containment approach can proceed without inviting a blow back. (This is a feature that notably did not obtain during the Cold War with the Soviet Union.) China, and not the US, is now the largest trading partner of most countries in the region, Australia and Russia included, with long term trade deficits with ASEAN, South Korea, Japan, and Australia. In other words, China is the leading buyer of their goods, and they would be loathe to annoy it for that reason alone, leaving aside broader macro factors such as the large differential in size, population, power potential etc. The Chinese media never fails to underscore this aspect—the overall beneficial impact of China's growing economy on them all, not to mention direct 'gives' such as the recently established 3 billion yuan (US$ 500 million approx.) China ASEAN Maritime Cooperation Fund—secure in the knowledge that it is the one that enjoys the upper hand, in the final analysis, as a large totalitarian state with staying power and capacity to bend the 'mutual dependence' of an inter-dependent relationship into 'one-sided leverage' to its advantage. Not surprisingly, fears of outbreak of protectionism stemming from trade related conflicts abound, resulting in most countries in the region hedging their bets and 'watching warily'.

That brings us to the next point about the responsiveness to the new policy of the US' partners. ASEAN's opportunism—seeking to enjoy the benefits of security free, as a 'public good' provided by the US presence, without themselves coming out into the open, as it were—is well known, as is ASEAN proclivity for avoiding a confrontational approach. According to one account (in the journal Comparative Connections), a draft of the ASEAN-US Joint Statement after their second Summit in New York in September 2010 that leaked out had contained references to the South China Sea dispute and non-use of force. It was whittled down to leave only a general note on the importance of 'regional peace and stability, maritime security, freedom of navigation and peaceful settlement of disputes' in the final version adopted, after a Chinese Foreign Ministry spokesman had warned against 'any kind of statement that might be issued by the US and ASEAN over the South China Sea'. The US release did, however, make explicit mention of non-use of force in the South China Sea, betraying the open secret about ASEAN being the side that had chickened out.

US media reports and commentators frequently claim ASEAN countries privately press the US to intervene on the South China issue. Lieberthal, amongst others, has written that 'the United States' initiatives apparently received warm vocal support from nearly all major countries at the (latest) East Asia Summit'. These claims will need to be checked by our diplomacy – and we can be sure that this is being done—in order to enable independent assessments in this regard.

Finally, there is the factor of the likely Chinese responses that would need to be grappled with in any such reckoning of the US strategic posture, assuming the US does manage to get its economic act together, overcoming these constraints and uncertainties. All available evidence (regarding Chinese reactions to the shift in the US approach), and expertise within the country on China, would need to be drawn upon to fathom their intentions and response. It is obviously very important for analysts in India to be able to figure that out in order to be able to correctly anticipate the shape of things to come in their entirety, and ensure careful calibration of our own stance accordingly.

The immediate Chinese reaction to the US (and 11 other) statements at the Hanoi ARF in July 2010 was, we know from a number of media reports, uncharacteristically unrestrained—the Chinese Foreign Minister Yang Jiechi, clearly caught unawares, was reported to have not been able to control his anger at the ganging up against China and at US success in rallying ASEAN and other countries (not to speak of its managing to bring up the sovereignty issue at that forum, which China had succeeded in warding off from its agenda hitherto).

According to one reliable account, he stared at the Singapore representative (the Foreign Minster) before blurting out 'China is a big country and other countries are small and that is just a fact'. Such display of ire, though not common for the Chinese, is not surprising because for them, this was a manifestation of their biggest nightmare—the dreaded multilateral consolidation against China! It might have been the first time he was confronted with the consequences of his country's gaucherie assertiveness that had been gathering momentum over several months; so, it is understandable that he may have lost control of himself in a state of shock. (The Chinese Ministry of Foreign Affairs website reportedly took pains to weave a coherent account around Yang Jiechi's intemperate remarks two days later. I am sorry to have not had an opportunity to go into that tangled web for it would surely have made interesting reading.)

At the (first) ASEAN Defence Ministers' meeting with the 'Plus Eight' countries,

ASEAN Defence Ministers' Meeting - Plus (ADMM+), in Hanoi in October that year, the South China Sea disputes were again brought up by 8 members. The Chinese representative (Defence Minister) reportedly reacted only mildly, though before the meeting he had been reported to be insistent that the ADMM+ was not the right forum for discussing the problem. More tellingly, Chinese Vice Foreign Minister, Zhang Zhijun, was dispatched to four South East Asian countries reportedly on a 'listening cum reassurance' mission in that same month, and Vice-President Xi Jinping to Singapore in November on the occasion of the 20th anniversary of diplomatic relations, where he notably made his 'China sees all countries, big and small, as equals' remark; no doubt in a bid to undo the Hanoi ARF damage wrought by his Foreign Minister.

These immediate reactions apart, the Chinese approach to the new US posture of 2010 and policy announcements of late 2011 appears to have evolved, reflecting a possible recognition that hammering on the containment theme frontally, in confrontationist terms, could prove to be counter-productive. Official and quasi-official media coverage has of late, at least, been low key, playing down the conflictual conceptual underpinnings of the new US posture. Sometimes, the latter has even been projected in almost benign terms—as 'more a case of strengthening Washington's influence in the area than specifically targeting China' or even as a strategy for 'elevating economic statecraft as a pillar of American foreign policy' (i.e. for refurbishing the economy, rather than beefing up security—choosing to take a remark in Clinton's article in 'Foreign Policy' to that effect at face value). Some of the Xinhua and English language media (aimed at foreign audiences) reports over this last week-end, on Obama's remarks (while releasing the latest DSR last week) vowing to 'strengthen the US presence in the Asia-Pacific', would seem to be in the same vein. Largely neutral, some went to the extent of acknowledging the 'legitimate interests of the US in the Asia-Pacific region' and welcoming it (the US) to 'make more contributions to peace and stability in the Asia-Pacific' (emphasis added) while cautioning it, of course, against 'recklessly practis(ing) militarism in the region' and to 'abstain from flexing its muscles'.

It is notable in this connection that the official and other State controlled media has been projecting US-China military ties as improving, post Hu

Jintao's visit to the US in January 2011, pointing to the exchange of high level defence officials' visits over the course of the year. So also for the overall bilateral relationship, where the 'impressive level of institutionalisation' through 60 plus bilateral mechanisms is noted for imparting it stability.

At the same time, the other strand—a hard-line, calling for fitting responses by way of strengthened deterrence capabilities—is never entirely absent from the quasi-official media. It makes no bones about China's 'military rise' in the long run, while vigorously contesting the view that China will be a factor for instability in the region. This tack openly questions US capacity to sustain the containment approach, daring it to go beyond mere verbal support and provide more economic benefits to the smaller nations it wishes to enlist in an anti-China alliance. ('China has more resources to oppose the US ambition of dominating the region than the US has of to fulfill it'.) Even the official media is blasé about noting the fact that the US needs China's goodwill and cooperation on a whole host of issues globally.

It would, thus, appear that no definitive decisions have been taken by the top leadership in China as yet as to how best to tackle the gathering storm to prevent the worst-case scenarios from materialising, while naturally preparing for them militarily without losing time. No categorical conclusions can therefore perhaps be drawn about the state of play within that country in respect of perceptions of, and response to, the new US posture, beyond the obviously anticipatable one of a strong sense of unease and confusion at the wholly unwelcome prospect of isolation.

On the other hand, it is clear that the China too, like the US, hardly enjoys a free hand. Its heavily export dependent economy (30% of GDP) has its own share of troubles, compelled to cope as it is with weakening demand in most of its markets in the industrialised world. Its property market is believed to be on a bubble waiting to burst, unless it can somehow pull through the miracle of a soft landing. Its banks are known to be saddled with bad debts. And its model (of export and State investment driven, 'extensive', growth) is under strain, and slated to be overhauled, avowedly, under the structural transformation envisaged in the 12th Plan in favour of one based on more 'intensive', and domestic consumption demand driven, growth. Many economists warn that affecting such structural adjustment is not going to be easy. And acute socio-economic inequalities (which incidentally is highest in the world in China, with a Gini coefficient greater than even that in the US), and problems of misuse of authority, have led to a steep rise in unrest and tensions (1,80,000 'mass incidents' in 2010, as per official figures), fuelled by the new digital social media despite all attempts by the authorities to control and limit its impact.

[Public opinion is fast becoming—or perhaps has already become—a volatile, almost uncontrollable, variable, especially on governance issues impacting upon people's livelihood directly, where the numbers involved are much larger and the fearlessness stronger. Tight control is—has per force to be—limited to macro-political issues of a systemic nature, for example, democracy, that concern intellectuals more than the citizenry at large. While little information is available on the impact of the digital media led, or facilitated, spontaneous political movements in the Arab world (and elsewhere) in terms of emboldening Chinese (netizen) public opinion, it may not be far-fetched to surmise that these examples would be giving nightmares to the Chinese leadership, which by all accounts has no answers (in its repressive repertoire, but also ideologically) to self-immolations (as by monks and nuns in Tibet) that mock at its attempt to rally the populace around the idea of a 'harmonious' society.]

Thus, there is no dearth of 'wild cards', and the mere possibility of their interplay with subterranean, nationalist or other potentially incendiary, sentiments getting out of hand should make for caution and restraint amongst the political class/Party as a whole while formulating a response to the new US strategic posture, particularly in the run up to the Party Congress due later this year. But that is a real imponderable—things could just as well take a diametrically opposite turn, taking even seasoned China watchers by surprise, as has happened in the past—especially if the Americans were to up the ante at any stage and seek to play on their (China's) vulnerabilities in a more direct manner, for example, in any future burgeoning 'Chinese spring'.

Overall, the jury is, and likely will remain, out on the likely response of a 'rising China' to the changing external scenario: status quoist or revisionist? Official establishments may have their minds made up in this regard on the basis of their predisposed predilections but in the academia, the debate between 'optimist liberals' and 'pessimist realists', as they are often described in graphic terms, will perhaps continue as long as the fault-lines remain inexplicit, as they are likely to.

The former (liberals), it has been argued, will maintain that China's rising aspirations can be accommodated through incremental change in the current international order characterised, in their opinion, by increasing economic and political openness (even if a trifle too slowly, most of them will concede). And that, so long as that remains the case, China is likely to gradually step into the role of the 'responsible stakeholder' that the US envisages for it, rather than venture to overturn the system and establish an order more to its own liking (resentful of being constricted to be a 'rule taker') even as it seeks to alter some rules of the game, wherever feasible, to redress (perceived historical) disadvantage.

The latter (realists), on the other hand, have generally been considered unready to accept any such sanguine prognosis, in view of the record of Chinese assertiveness already witnessed since 2009, and even more, of the way that record is stoutly defended in much of the quasi official Track II literature emanating from China (which does not seem to consider it necessary to re-think, or question, the rather extravagant premises—about core interests etc. —on which China's assertive actions appear to have been based, even while counseling moderation internally in recognition of the adverse impact of such behavior on China tactically). There is little or no sign of realisation that China's plight (of being confronted with the US 'strategic turn to the Asia-Pacific region' as the 'heart of our foreign policy', in the words of US Secretary of State, Hillary Clinton) and the prospect of diplomatic isolation is largely self-invited.

Two recent writings, which I happen to have come across would seem to be worthy of follow up attention and enquiry in this context, in my opinion, amongst others—a Report titled '*Constructing an Orderly International System: Trends, Turmoil and Principles for Maintaining Order*' reported to have been released by the Institute of Modern International Relations, Tsinghua University in December last, and a speech by the Director of the Institute of World Economics and Politics, Chinese Academy of Social

Sciences, Zhang Yuyuan, reported again by the Global Times around the same time. Both cogitate upon the existing, and changing, international order: the capacity, or lack of it, of present day international institutions for solving problems with reference to the question of 'responsibilities and rights' of states The latter, introducing the term 're-globalisation'—as the new trend it claims was ushered in during 2011 (with the connotation of it being possible to start afresh, on a clean slate, as it were)—concludes that 'reglobalisation means setting new international rules, and the power of rule-making will become the focus of future competition', and that China should make good use of it.

What about the implications for India? This is naturally the question of greatest interest but one that, I would submit, deserves to be the subject of a fuller discussion, perhaps as the theme of another seminar taking off from this one. So I will limit myself to offering just a few preliminary thoughts, further to the concern referred to earlier (in paragraph 18), not to stray away too far from the theme of the seminar and mindful also of the time constraint.

There has been no official reaction to the new US posture, understandably, but it may be recalled that media reports had disclosed that India had no hesitation in endorsing 'freedom of navigation in international waters, including the South China Sea, and right of passage in accordance with accepted principles of international law' at the July 2010 Hanoi ASEAN Regional Forum (ARF). That forthright position was followed by firmness in rejecting Chinese attempts to object to, and prevent, Indian oil exploration in the waters off Vietnam's coast in 2011. The Chinese PM raised the matter with Indian Prime Minister Dr. Manmohan Singh during their meeting on the side-lines of the East Asia Summit in November last, only to receive a reiteration of the earlier firm official level response in more polite language. (Those habitually hawking a 'pro-active' stance by India, mirroring the perceived 'offensive defence' approach of China for paying China back in its own coin—with or without ripened objective conditionswould have taken note hopefully.)

The proclaimed US policy posture does hold the promise of introduction of an entirely new element in India's strategic calculus—obviously. One that has the potential of redefining the landscape, subject to the several caveats mentioned earlier. But this needs to be understood in perspective, and without going overboard. Superficial, or jingoistic, interpretations explicating its possible implications in simplistic 'balance of power' terms (as happened in the media during the public debate on the India-US Civil Nuclear Cooperation Agreement), must be eschewed for freewheeling or casual strategising invariably ends up doing great disservice to the nation.

'Strategic reticence', as befitting a mature polity capable of strategising in a sober manner with a sense of realism and restraint, would appear to be the call of the day. Together with an in-depth, on-going, focus on the military and economic dimensions of the evolving Sino-US equation, not only inside but also outside Government, to promote deeper understanding of both the points of conflict as well as the leverages available to each against the other. That would hold the key to identification of optimal options open to the nation in each specific circumstance of these two countries locking horns.

Benefiting from the potentially favourable currents may not be easy, paradoxically, for reasons to do as much with systemic inertia and languor at our own end as much as external factors. Public opinion would need to be brought up to date, and encouraged to give up the shibboleths of an era gone by, if opportunities are not to be wasted. Overcoming that mind-set will call for tremendous agility and alacrity, both institutional and intellectual, for charting untested waters in a strategic environment in a state of continuous flux, lacking the fixities and certitudes of the past. Moreover, the opportunities will not be available as low hanging fruit, as would appear (to be the expectation) from the tenor of some of the discussion in the public discourse. The new scenario is likely to present hard choices—sharp trade-offs, in the language of managerial economics, entailing realisation that some gains can be had only at the cost of others—a concept which is not always accorded due weightage in the public debate. That, in turn, requires a broad consensus across the political spectrum on sharpened prioritization of national interests and long term goals—a tall order in the best of times. Also that the potential gains are likely to come with heightened risks—risks as are inherent in every opportunity—which will need to be weighed and evaluated in the light of the overall situation prevailing at any given time on a case by case basis.

Externally, the challenge of being able to steer an independent course, without getting caught in cross-fire, in the face of possible polarising rhetoric from one end, and its likely rejection at the other end on the basis of invocation of unexceptionable principles (sanctity of sovereignty, resolution of disputes by direct negotiations between the countries concerned free of interference by extra regional powers, opposition to military bases outside one's own territory, right to equity based political space for development, etc.) could prove to be formidable. Ironically, an explicit ideological or — normative fault line (such as democracy) might have made the task in this respect easierthe absence of an overt, demonstrably defensive, framework for coordinated action hands propaganda advantage to the 'contain-ee' (placing the 'containing' side in the docks *ipso facto* for an old style, Cold war kind combative, approach to security and inter-state relations). The 'complexities of congruence' in the new Cold War period, prematurely beginning to be termed by some as the 'post-post-Cold war era', could thus prove to be more daunting than the challenges of the period of 'estrangement' of the largest and the oldest democracies.

A cautious welcome and dispassionate consideration, to the opportunities opening up before the country would, therefore, seem to recommend itself. These are early days, and a 'Watch and Wait' (WAW) approach to allow the dust raised by incipient trends to settle down may be in order. 2012 will in any case be a political transition year, not only within the two principal antagonists' in the region but also in Russia, ROK, Taiwan, and the DPRK. (Iran, which like China is firmly on the US firmament, too possibly, with the impending Parliamentary elections.)

So also Thailand, awaiting the return of former PM Shinawatra.) Moreover, it is being labeled as a 'make or break' year for the global economy, in which most nations are likely to await the outcome of the US efforts at recovery of its economy before casting their lot one way or the other, if at all.

In sum, classic 'masterly inactivity'… or, to put it another way, taking a leaf out Lao Tse, "The perfect practitioner appears to do nothing, yet ensures that nothing is left undone."

Index